the

FAMILY BLESSING

guidebook

ISBN 978-0-9783947-2-1

www.powerofblessing.com

For more information email
info@powerofblessing.com

TABLE OF CONTENTS

ACKNOWLEDGEMENTS

Rolf Garborg, our friend and mentor in publishing. Rolf is also the author of The Family Blessing, a book with a similar title to this one. It contains a captivating message of how family blessing was woven into the fabric of Rolf's family over many years. Available from Summerside Press
www.summersidepress.com

Alf Davis, an amazing counselor whose insight and personal assistance have proven invaluable to the formation and communication of our message. Alf's insights on personal wholeness and transformation are freely available at
www.lovehealstv.com

Craig Hill, founder of Family Foundations International whose book The Ancient Paths contains the initial inspiration for our teaching on the seven crucial stages for family blessing.
www.familyfoundations.com

INTRODUCTION

This is *not* a self-help book.

This is a book that unlocks a forgotten talent that you can use in every one of your important relationships.

The practice of Family Blessing has been proven over centuries especially in the Jewish culture.

Today it has largely been lost or never learned.

We have devoted many years to learning and applying the power of blessing in our relationships with children, family, friends and even in our business life. We have tested this teaching in many different countries, cultures and languages on five separate continents. *We know it works.*

The Bible has been our guidebook in principle and in practice, yet at the same time, we have seen that that *Family Blessing is applicable to people of all faiths.*

While this book does not contain everything we teach, it does contain everything we think you need to know in order to give and receive family blessings at every stage of life. Our goal is not to merely teach concepts, but to assist you to recover your missed blessings and to learn how to give blessings to others. It's divided into three sections which offer you something for your HEAD, your HEART and your HAND.

Section ONE gets straight to the point. It explains what Family Blessing is and why it matters in your life.

Section TWO goes for the heart. It uses the power of stories to paint a clear picture of what Family Blessing looks like at every stage of life and *how to recover the blessings you have missed along the way.*

Section THREE shows you how to apply blessing to your important relationships. The Appendices put the tools in your hands.

We encourage you to *not* skip the first two sections for this reason: *You can't give what you haven't received!*

By taking the time to absorb the foundational concepts then reading through the seven stages, you will discover which blessings may still be missing from your life. Learning how to receive blessings you have missed, will increase your effectiveness when you bless others.

May the eyes of your heart be enlightened as you read these pages.
May you receive every blessing that you need and desire.
May you be inspired to bless others with deliberate words and actions.

Terry & Melissa Bone

PART ONE

Understanding the Power

CHAPTER 1

The Cry of Every Heart

"When Esau heard his father's words, he burst out with a loud and bitter cry and said to his father, Bless me – me too, my father... Then Esau wept aloud"

Genesis 27:34,*38b.*

BLESSING! What an overused word!

When we are in good health we call it a blessing. When an unexpected check comes in the mail, we call it a blessing. When we drive our car too fast and the person ahead of us gets caught for speeding instead of us, we call it a blessing.

Whenever life is pleasing us in any way we call it a blessing.

So, you may ask, what is a real blessing?

And what difference does it make in a person's life?

Blessing defined

There are several different kinds of blessings. Some are rewards for obedience. Some are material blessings. However, these are not the focus of this book.

When we use the term *blessing*, we are referring to what we call *Family Blessing.* These blessings are not rewards for obedience, they are rewards for being born! They are not earned, but rather *they are gifts from God.* They are spiritual not material. They do not immediately increase your bank account, but they do deposit *spiritual riches* into your heart.

Simply put, Family Blessings can be understood as God's favor poured into your life. *This kind of blessing empowers you to prosper so you can have a satisfying life journey.*

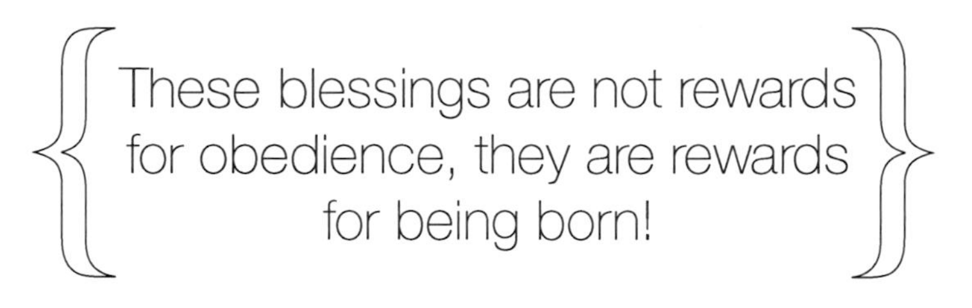

You were designed to be blessed
We all need this blessing regardless of our age, gender, or family circumstance. *Somewhere deep within, we all have an intense longing to receive spiritual blessing.*

It may be hidden under many other desires and pleasures, but it cannot be eradicated from our inner being. It's embedded in the spiritual DNA of every living person.

Our extensive travels have offered us first hand evidence that this heart cry is inherent in every human being. People everywhere respond to this message with hunger and passion. Whether among the poorest of the poor in a rural Asian village, or the upper middle class in urban California, the need for Family Blessing is readily evident in every language and culture.

Why is this so? *Because God designed us this way.*

It is essential to understand that God does not intend for any person to live without His blessing. In fact, God's very first act on behalf of the very first people on earth was to *speak a blessing* over them (see Genesis 1:28). These words were not merely words of encouragement, or a verbal "pat on the back" as Adam and Eve began their life.

On the contrary, the blessing they received contained spiritual power that enabled Adam and Eve to begin fulfilling their destiny as overseers of the earth and its inhabitants. It was not something they had to earn. It was a *free gift!* A gift that enabled the very first husband and wife team to love each other freely and to govern the earth effectively.

Adam and Eve forfeited this free gift (and much more) through their sinful disobedience. However God already had a plan, not only for the redemption of individuals, but also for the *restoration of families.*[1] He inaugurated this plan with a man called Abraham (see Genesis 12:1-3). The remaining 38 chapters of Genesis are entirely devoted to the story of how Abraham's blessing impacted four generations of his family and set the stage for future generations.

> God's very first act on behalf of the very first people on earth was to speak a blessing over them

A quick reading of these chapters reveals a recurring theme:

Spoken blessing, from parents to children, plays an important role in empowering the next generation to fulfill their life purpose.

The gift of "Family Blessing" became so coveted that Abraham's grandson Esau cried out in anguish when his father Isaac withheld it!

The *specific* blessing that was passed on between the generations of Abraham's descendents was unique. However the spiritual and relational dynamics associated with blessing still exists within families today. This is powerfully illustrated in the life of a man who never knew what he was missing until he found it.

When we met Doug he was a happily married man secure in his God-given purpose in life, yet there was a time when Doug's destiny was in question because of a missed blessing. In his own words:

> *My Father died in [the] Vietnam [war] when I was five years old. The last thing I expected was to receive a letter from him 17 years later. But that is what happened one winter day when I was 22 years old.*
>
> *It was the day my fiancée and I announced our engagement. I remember being in the kitchen alone that evening. My mother walked in and handed me a letter copied onto old mimeograph paper. The seven pages were still folded, evidence of an envelope since discarded.*
>
> *"What's this?" I asked. "It's something I should have given you years ago," my mother said. "It's a letter from your father. He wrote it to you from Vietnam soon after he arrived there, just in case something was to happen to him. He said that if he were not to return from the war, I was to give it to you when you became a man.... I realize that I should have given it to you a long time ago. I'm sorry."*
>
> *It is hard to describe how jolting her words were. I sat there stunned. Finally, after a few minutes, I managed to unfold the pages. They were hand written. It felt like a privilege to see his handwriting. I had not seen it before.*
>
> *Part of me was afraid to read it . . . afraid that – with one quarter of my life behind me – I would find it would not have pleased him...that I would not have his blessing.... I had adjusted to not having to take into account my father's approval or disapproval. Now, all of a sudden, I might have to. At the same time, I felt humbled that I was even getting the chance to know my father's thoughts.*
>
> *When I finished reading the letter, it was as if the weight of the world had been lifted from my shoulders. I was not faced with trying to rebuild my life, after all. Instead, my dad had*

affirmed me, citing traits he had seen in me even when I was a little boy. His words were encouraging and motivating, not scolding or dogmatic. He did not lecture or warn me, but simply shared his thoughts. Instead of trying to persuade me to follow in his footsteps (which I had begun to do – even applying to West Point [Military Academy], only to withdraw my application), he held up virtues for which I could strive no matter what career I chose. It felt good that, after all those years, I had some basis for thinking my dad would have been proud of me.

His letter had filled a place in my heart which I had only been semi-aware of and had no idea was so large. I had received my father's blessing... This man was a virtual stranger to me, even though I shared his genes. Yet, because he was my father, his attention and affirmation in a letter mailed a week before his death profoundly impacted the course of my life as an adult. He gave me permission to proceed in a direction I would have gone anyway, but now could go with greater confidence.[2]

The Power of Blessing will Impact Your Life

Doug's response perfectly describes the benefits of parental blessing upon a young adult:

- › confidence in his own character,
- › confirmation of life calling,
- › the lifting of an emotional weight from his soul.

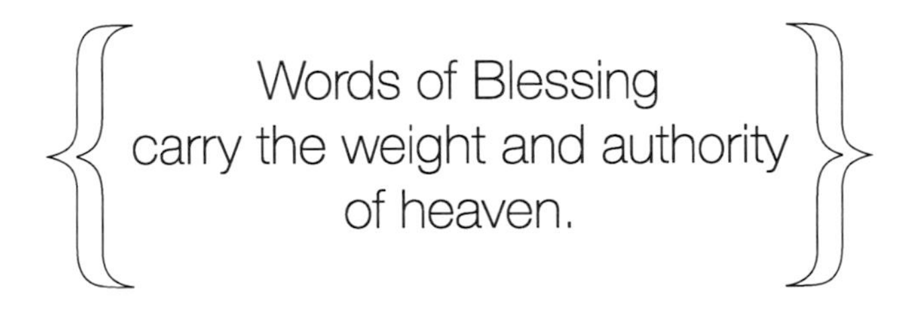

The cry in Doug's heart had been answered through a written blessing, received years after his father's death. Today it still has an impact on his life.

Your Family Blessing will impact your life as well!

As we'll demonstrate in later chapters, words of blessing carry the weight and authority of heaven. They impart life and hope, and change the way we think about ourselves. A blessing conveys heaven's perspective on who we are and where we are meant to go in life. We call that *identity* and *destiny. Words of blessing give us insight and spiritual ability to walk in the light of God's revealed will for our lives.*

God has delegated His authority to us to speak blessings on His behalf. That is especially true with respect to parents who are meant to impart a blessing to their children.

Very few of us, however, have a parent like Doug's father who was careful to plan ahead. So what happens if our parents are unable or unwilling to give us this blessing?

The unfortunate truth is that the majority of parents today are not fully aware how vital a blessing can be. We haven't been schooled in this subject and don't understand how to give this gift to our children. Neither do we have living examples to give us a picture of how it's done. As a result, *many of us limp through life without the Family Blessings we were meant to receive.*

The good news is, *you can recover the blessings you missed earlier in life.*

Ephesians 1:3 asserts that *God has* blessed us already in the heavenly places. It's as if there are countless packages stored in heaven's warehouse. Among them is a neatly arranged stack of packages with your name on them. Lovingly prepared by the heavenly Father with you in mind, they sit there waiting to be delivered to the door of your heart. If you were able to wander through that warehouse in heaven, you would notice that there is no expiry date on the packages.

It is never too late to recover your missed blessings! If the people (such as parents) who were supposed to deliver those packages to the door of your heart are unable or unwilling, God can bring someone else into your life to get the job done.

It is amazing to watch how quickly a person can move from merely *surviving* in life to *thriving* in life once these missed blessings are recovered. We have seen it happen countless times in the lives of people to whom we have ministered, whether one-on-one, or in a group seminar setting.

In the chapters that follow we will use many Bible stories and personal testimonies to help unfold the secrets to effective blessing. You will learn

› the seven crucial stages when everyone needs blessing,

› *how* to recover the blessings you have missed earlier in life and

› how to give a blessing to anyone who needs one.

We will take the time to clearly demonstrate *how* a blessing works.

But this we can assure you - it *DOES* work!
And it is one of the keys for fulfilling your destiny – your highest calling in life.

ENDNOTE 1 Expressed cryptically in Genesis 3:15 is the idea and plan of redemption – victory over the 'serpent' i.e. Satan through the 'seed' of the woman i.e. Jesus Christ. We believe that the story of sin and eternal redemption is the foundation for all scripture but we are limiting our discussion of the scriptures to the theme of family blessing and how it impacts our lives here on earth.

ENDNOTE 2 Copyright J. Doug Burford. Used with permission. The unedited version of this story can be found in Jack Canfield and Mark Victor Hansen's book *Chicken Soup for the Christian Family Soul.* Health Communications Inc. Deerfield Beach, Florida, 2000, pg. 89

CHAPTER 2

Living Without the Blessing

"Few people see themselves as struggling with missing out on their family's blessing, but people around them see it."

Genesis 27:41a

Esau was more than 40 years old. He was a married man with children of his own, yet he wept like a little child because his father would not lay his hands on his head and bless him.

Esau knew the stories of God's promise to Abraham, his grandfather. He was aware of how God had appeared to his grandfather and to his father, and he longed for the day that the family blessing God imparted to them could be passed on to him.

Esau was grief stricken at the thought of trying to live the rest of his adult life without it.

He knew that without that blessing he would have no access to the rich storehouse of promises made to his grandfather Abraham.

He knew that *without the blessing*, he would not prosper in spite of his talents. He also knew that *with* the blessing, his brother Jacob *would* prosper in spite of his faults.

And so he wept. He wept for what could have been but now was beyond his reach.

The denial of this blessing affected Esau's behaviour for decades and his family for generations.

It "bent" his relationships with family members: he turned away from his brother Jacob in hatred (see Genesis 27:41) and turned toward his parents in vain attempts to win their approval (see Genesis 26:34, 28:8-9).

Compensation is not a cure

Few of us today value parental blessing as much as these two brothers did, however *we cannot escape the effect of its absence.* Whether we realize it or not, when a parent's blessing is withheld, the vast majority of us will tend to adopt certain relationship patterns in an attempt to compensate for missed blessings. Our personalities become "bent" – i.e. shaped by unsuccessful attempts to fill a void that we feel but can't define.

Three of the most common ways in which people "bend" to achieve the missed blessing are through *aggression, agreement*, and *performance orientation*. These are illustrated by the family experience of a woman we encountered at a retreat. Our teaching helped her understand why she and her two sisters were so different from each other even though they had experienced the same family misfortune. In her own words:

> *Our father was very conniving. Always wanting a boy, he basically undermined us as growing women. I got angry. My tendency now is violent anger toward any hurt or injustice. The second child is still so in agreement with the identity put on her, that to this day she has bouts of depression requiring her to take a few days off at a time just for restoration. The youngest went a different direction. She has read all the books (on self-improvement) and has determined to be the nicest person out there."*

> when a parent's blessing is withheld, the majority of us will tend to adopt certain relationship patterns in an attempt to compensate

Let's take a closer look at these three patterns and how they block our pathway to emotional wholeness.

Aggression: In attempting to reject the rejection they have experienced, people develop a pattern of aggression. They may become defiant, stubborn, cynical, and critical of others, and they may rebel against authority or refuse comfort. A saying that seems applicable here is, *They are trying to fight fire with fire.* This refers to the tactic of stopping an advancing forest fire by lighting a fire moving toward it in the opposite direction. Too often the unintended result is merely the creation of a bigger fire. The angry person often believes that his or her best defense against the approaching "fire" of criticism or rejection is to speak aggressively towards others. The fact of the matter is that you cannot solve criticism with a critical attitude. Nor can you cure the pain of being cursed by cursing others.

Not everyone in this category is outwardly angry. Aggression is not always overt. Some people use "the silent treatment" as a weapon of control or revenge. This is called being *passive aggressive.* This kind of aggression is harder to recognize, but it has the same root of anger and ultimately produces the same bad fruit in a person's character.

Agreement: Persons who come into agreement with the lack of blessing may hear themselves thinking thoughts of inferiority and failure. They might also suffer from anxiety and low self esteem. You can recognize this kind of person by the way they constantly put themselves down with their own words. The people who are in agreement with a false and negative identity are prone to constant comparisons of themselves with others. Inevitably these comparisons leave them ever more convinced of their lack of talent and worth.

You can also recognize these people by their *inability to receive a compliment*. They cannot just say thank you when someone praises them. They will always feel the need to respond with a reminder of how they are flawed in some other way. This behavior pattern masquerades as humility but it's not. True humility comes from an accurate assessment of your own limits. A truly humble person possesses a quiet confidence that makes no demand for personal attention.

Performance Orientation: A common way to compensate for the lack of blessing is to become performance oriented; constantly striving, compulsive, self-centered or self-absorbed. Many adopt this pattern of compensation for missed blessings because *people affirm them in their good works*. The doers of good works believe that their drivenness is a sign of character and moral strength. The attention and praise they receive from others, especially those in authority, strengthens this belief. Often these people become over-achievers in their careers, setting sales records or rising to the top positions in their corporation. In spite of great achievements these people often exhibit signs of emotionally immaturity. Their noteworthy accomplishments do no more to fill the blessing gap in their soul than wallpapering a hole in the wall fixes the wall. It looks good on the surface until you apply a little pressure!

> any kind of performance orientation will consign you to live inside the borders of a land called 'Never Enough'

It needs to be stated here that religious homes are especially vulnerable to a special kind of performance orientation that can block the blessing – *striving for good behavior in the name of serving God*.

Children with a strong religious upbringing may remain fiercely loyal to their parents who strive for moral perfection. The parents may look like a shining example of good works. They may engage in tireless efforts for a noteworthy cause. Yet their laudable actions are driven by an unseen and unmet need for affirmation. Though very religious, these people usually fail to grasp the all-important distinction between love and approval. Expressions of love and affirmation are limited to occasions when their child performs to a high standard. As a result, the intended family blessing is blocked. These children are inhibited from experiencing the true joy of being loved for *who they are* and not just for *what they do*. Consequently they may become adults who falsely believe that God's love is conditional upon good performance.

Religion-based or not, *any kind of performance orientation* will consign you to live inside the borders of a land called "Never Enough." You will constantly strive, but the elusive blessing will remain just beyond your reach like the carrot dangling in front of the proverbial donkey that keeps moving forward trying to reach it.

A false sense of success

Sometimes the lack of Family Blessing is ignored or minimized when a person achieves great success. When aggression is combined with performance orientation it produces a mix that is 'high octane' but toxic to the soul.

This pattern can often be recognized in the lives of famous persons, especially professional athletes. Lance Armstrong was at one time considered the world's greatest long distance cyclist and a hero to many for his accomplishments as a cancer survivor.

Long before performance-enhancing drugs were commonly used in his sport, Lance demonstrated an astonishing level of mental and physical toughness that produced phenomenal results. As a teenager, Lance won almost every race he entered. In addition to natural gifting and excellent training, **he credits his early successes to the fact that he was an angry young man:** "*I would win on adrenaline and anger, chopping off my competitors one by one. I could push myself to a threshold of pain no one else was willing to match, and I would bite off somebody's head off to win a race.*"[1]

Lance revealed that the source of the anger that motivated him to succeed was connected to emotional pain from his past. Lance never knew his biological father. And the man that his mom welcomed into their home as husband and stepfather abused both of them.

Candidly he admits:

"*You don't want to think about your adolescent resentments when you're trying to make a 6,500-foot climb... But that said, it's all stoked down in there, fuel for the fire... the old wounds and long-ago slights become the stuff of competitive energy.*"[2]

Lance had learned how to channel his anger into a furious motivation that produced phenomenal achievements and (for a period of time) earned him fame and fortune.

But don't mistake great achievements for a happy and blessed life. After his second Tour de France victory, Lance wrote a book in which he wrote glowingly about his (first) wife who had stood by him through all his trials. The book concludes with Lance saying, "*...we celebrated the fact that there would be other races ...And then we went home to Austin as a family, happily*"[3]. Ultimately this kind of 'happily ever after' scenario was unattainable for Lance. He lost both his marriage and his Tour titles.[4]

One psychiatrist summed it up with these words "*Armstrong's truth ...is that his father abandoned him at age 2. Two years old...is plenty old enough to set the stage for a decades-long race for enough fame and fortune to fill the emotional back hole inside you that keeps threatening to make you disappear into it*"[5]

You can also see a similar dynamic at work in the life of some well-known Christian leaders who create huge ministries and seem to have boundless energy for non-stop growth in their organizations. Yet in spite of being touted as models for us to follow, they often pay a personal price for their 'drivenness' that includes family breakdowns. Some also experience lapses of integrity, which bring ruin to their ministries and deep disillusionment to their followers.

We don't share these thoughts to be critical of anyone. Every person has faults and, for most of us, they remain hidden from public view. But don't be fooled by the apparent success of anyone who denies the need to address the pain from their past. No amount of accomplishment in life can overcome an emotional deficit in your soul! Family Blessings are always a required element in the process of becoming whole.

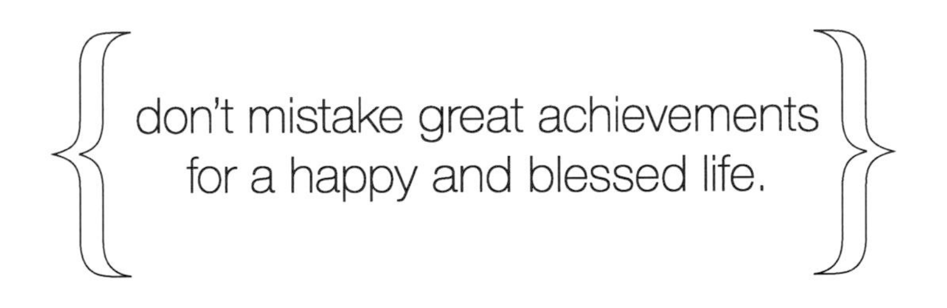

A false sense of failure

A far more common result of performance orientation than a world record in cycling is the scenario of the *failed perfectionist*. We are referring to persons who set themselves up for failure by attempting to achieve unrealistic expectations. Typically these are people who have sensitive hearts. They want to do what is best, but become entangled in a "no-win" situation due to the lack of affirmation and blessing.

A poignant illustration came in the form of an email from Laura[6] who told us she had waited all her life for a blessing from her father. From her earliest years she had tried to please him to no avail. Her efforts to carry his tools to the construction site at the tender age of eight didn't win his approval. Nothing she did worked. And to make matters worse, each time she failed to measure up to her father's expectations, he responded with verbal abuse.

Throughout her teen years, Laura was an average student. She made heroic efforts, however, to win her parents' approval. Having scored 97 percent on a high school exam, she proudly presented her paper to her father. "Where are the other three marks?" he demanded. From that moment, everything changed.

Totally defeated, Laura gave up. Something within her died. For the next seven years she was caught in a downward spiral of alcohol and broken relationships. She became pregnant and aborted the child. In her mid-20's Laura found forgiveness, peace and hope in Jesus Christ. When she became a Christian she was rescued from harmful addictions through the power of God's Spirit. Her behavior changed, but she confessed that 25 years later she still had a longing deep inside to hear the words, well done, from her father. The Father's Blessing she so desperately craved still eluded her.

Laura experienced more personal pain when her husband died suddenly. For the next year she managed to keep her household running as a single mom. In a sudden shift of behavior, Laura's 82-year-old father surprised her with a phone call to tell her that he was proud of how she had taken care of everything in the past year.

Rather than being resentful, Laura was thankful. She had finally received a small taste of what she had longed for all her life. She told us that the phone call from dad "was like a cool breeze on a hot summer day, or a sip of water when I'm parched. I waited so long to hear those words, and I am so thankful they were spoken before he died."

"Walking wounded"

Without blessing we are the "walking wounded" carrying with us pain from the past while we try to get on with our lives. However *your* life story does not have to mirror any of the stories you have just read.

Unlike Esau, you do not need to spend the rest of your life in remorse over what could have been. *Unlike Lance*, you do not need to become a world champion in a vain attempt to overcome a painful past. *Unlike Laura* you do not need to be satisfied with one small drop of approval after a lifetime of longing.

Why? *It's because your blessings are still waiting for you!*

God has designed you to be blessed at every stage of your life journey. There are seven times when receiving a Family Blessing is crucial for shaping identity and downloading destiny. Let's find out how blessings are imparted at each stage, and how to get the ones we have missed along the way.

ENDNOTE 1 Page 65 Lance Armstrong, It's Not About the Bike, copyright 2000, Berkley Books New York NY

ENDNOTE 2 Page 20-21 Lance Armstrong, It's Not About the Bike, copyright 2000, Berkley Books, New York N.Y.

ENDNOTE 3 Page 289 Lance Armstrong, It's Not About the Bike, copyright 2000, Berkley Books, New York N.Y.

ENDNOTE 4 Lance's seven Tour de France titles were revoked in 2012 after former teammates testified that he had participated in the banned practice of "blood doping" which is commonly used by professional cyclists to boost their endurance and performance.

ENDNOTE 5 Excerpted from Will Lance Armstrong ever fess up and face the truth?
By Dr. Keith Ablow
Published October 23, 2012, Fox News.com The full article is worth the read. At the time of writing you could find it at www.foxnews.com/archive/author/dr-keith-ablow/index.html

ENDNOTE 6 *For most of the stories in this book we have changed the names but kept the story line accurate*

CHAPTER THREE

Border Crossings

...Thus conscious that I do exist,
In time's eternal plan,
O grant that I may know at least,
Why I was made a man.

From the Poem 'My Plea' by Thornton Hayward

We live in the beautiful Niagara Peninsula, about 30 minutes drive from one of the main border crossings between the U.S.A. and Canada. Like four million other Canadians in the region, we often travel between the two friendly nations for a variety of reasons. After crossing the Niagara River bridge, we are subjected to a series of questions posed by uniformed officials. Our journey is delayed until we provide believable answers. The first two questions always have to do with our identity:

"What is your citizenship?"
"Where do you live?"

In these days of identity theft and perceived terrorist threats, proof of I.D. is required usually in the form of a passport.

But that's not all. The questions sure to follow are more difficult to prove:

"Where are you going?"
"What is your purpose for going there?"

Until we convince the unsmiling official that we know where we are going and have a good reason for going there, *we won't be permitted to cross the border.*

your true identity cannot be self-invented,
it must be sovereignly revealed.

The same is true in life. There are key transition points in everyone's life journey at which we must stop and address the questions, Who am I, and Where am I going. Our life's journey is delayed until we provide satisfactory answers. These transition points are like emotional border crossings that require a firm understanding of our true identity and our correct destiny. We'll describe seven of them. But first let's have a closer look at what we mean by the terms *identity* and *destiny.*

Discovering your true identity

Who am I? Your identity is what makes you unique in this world. Without a relationship with your Creator, your identity will likely become a product of your family experience, your personality and your own invention.

But your true identity cannot be *self-invented.* It must be *sovereignly revealed.*

Your true identity flows from the heart of a loving heavenly Father:

- › what He knows about you,
- › the potential He sees in you,
- › the words He wants to speak to you.

When given as they should be, the Family Blessings help reveal and reinforce who God says you are rather than supporting the self-image you have created.

Discovering your divine destiny

Where am I going? At key transition points in life you also must answer the questions, Where am I going, and What is my purpose for going there. After all, your destination defines the purpose of your journey.

The word *destination* comes from the same root word as *destiny*. Perhaps you accept the dictionary definition that describes destiny as "a pre-determined course of events to which a person is assigned by fate." Or maybe you subscribe to the belief that your destiny is firmly in your own hands determined by your own efforts and choices. Neither is correct.

Destiny is not something you create yourself, nor is it arbitrarily assigned by an impersonal power called *fate*. Your destiny is a *designer version.*

God has pictured a special future for you. He knows exactly what He intends for you to accomplish in life. Your destiny is waiting for you. It's much larger than you have ever imagined, and getting there requires your involvement. You will need to make many good and godly choices along the way, but you will never fulfill all you were designed to be by your own effort or good works. You need the enabling power of blessing at every crucial "border crossing" in your journey.

Seven border crossings explained

Author Craig Hill describes seven crucial stages in life when blessing is required for the impartation of a sense of identity and destiny.[1] We have come to picture these transitions as "border crossings" where we must address major life questions in order to move successfully into the next phase.

> If Jesus required family blessings at each transition in his earthly life, how much more do we?

The only two people on earth who didn't need blessing to move from one phase of life to another were Adam and Eve. They were uniquely different from the rest of us. They were the only two people without belly-buttons! (*think about it for a minute...*) In other words, they were not born. They were created as adults and were not subject to the stages of life. God imparted the full measure of blessing to them in their full-grown state.

Everyone since Adam and Eve, including Jesus, was born into the world through a woman's womb. A full understanding of identity or destiny isn't imparted to us in a moment's time as it was to Adam and Eve. We acquire knowledge of our destiny more gradually as we progress through the major stages of development from conception, pregnancy and birth, through early childhood and teen years, and on to adulthood and senior years. At each stage God has assigned certain persons, especially parents, to bless us through words, deeds and ceremonies.

When present, these blessings become divine deposits in our hearts, and represent essential affirmation about who we are and where we are going. When we possess them in abundance, we prosper in life without striving. When they are absent, we struggle in life in spite of our valiant efforts.

Here's a compelling thought: If Jesus required the Family Blessings at each transition point in his earthly life, how much more do we?

We were pleased to discover that the gospels of Matthew and Luke record the first six of these crucial transitions in the life of Jesus. Though brief, these accounts reveal astounding truths about how Family Blessing works, especially in the earlier stages.

By now we can hear you asking, So, what are these border crossings and what do I need to know at each one? Let's have a look.

We have developed a series of life-questions that correspond to each stage. These questions will help you determine the divine deposit of blessing you need at each developmental stage in order to become fully blessed.

Stage of life	Major life questions
1. ***Conception***	Am I welcome in this world?
2. ***Pregnancy***	Where is a safe place for me in the world?
3. ***Birth***	Will my needs be met in this world?
4. ***Early Childhood***	Who can I trust in this world?
5. ***Teen Years***	Do I have what it takes to make it in this world?
6. ***Adulthood***	What am I called to do in this world and who will share my journey?
7. ***Senior Years***	Am I still needed in this world?

Conception: Am I welcome in this world? Seeds of acceptance or rejection are sown at conception. How you were conceived, and how your parents received the news of your conception are powerful factors in shaping your sense of identity.

Therefore the first time you need a blessing is the moment the announcement comes that your mother is "expecting". We like to say that your life begins on your "earth day" rather than on your birthday. By "earth day," we mean the moment when your spirit was somehow joined with the tiny, but growing, embryo within your mother's womb. From this moment you had life and your spirit needed to be blessed.

Think of what you need when you arrive for the first time as a student in a new classroom or as a guest at a social event. Your immediate need is to be recognized and welcomed. Feeling unwelcome affects your entire experience afterward. In the same way, the very first blessing you need is a warm welcome into this world as your body and soul begin to take shape.

Pregnancy: Where is a safe place for me in this world? The second time we need a blessing is during our months as a pre-born child.

Recent studies provide evidence of a fact which most mothers perceive intuitively – that pre-born children are affected by their mother's emotions, good or bad. The "fear factor" in life can show up even before our birthday. Thus the home environment as well as the mental, physical and emotional state of a mother impacts the answer to this life-question for the baby she carries.

Birth: Will my needs be met in this world? Before you understand your parents' language, you learn from experience. How you are held, touched, fed; the words you hear, and the manner in which they are spoken teach you whether or not your needs will be met in life.

Early childhood: Who can I trust in this world? That's the question of a child reaching out to others. From toddler to pre-teen you learn which relationships are safe and which are not. A foundation of basic trust needs to be poured into your personality during those years for you to grow in relationships later in life.

Teen years: Do I have what it takes to make it in this world? Puberty brings the biggest transition since conception. At the beginning of your teen years you need to know whether you have what it takes to make it. This question is a powerful driving force that *must* be answered for you to develop the emotional maturity and confidence that makes it possible for you to transition into the next phase of life.

Adulthood: The adult stage is really a series of smaller steps connected to form the story of career, calling and companions.

Over the past few years we have ministered to many young adults in various countries. The question they ask most often is, ***What am I called to do in life?*** To find and fulfill a life calling is a daunting prospect for many during these early adult years. And as they embark on this quest, a companion question arises:

Who will share my journey?
Creating and maintaining shared dreams for the future can be an elusive goal. For example, more than a few people are married to someone who does not share their spiritual journey. Also many are single by choice or by chance. Regardless of your marital status, God's intention to bless you includes the companionship of one or two close friends who understand and celebrate your life and dreams for the future.

Senior years: Am I still needed in this world? Everyone who has reached their senior years needs to know that they are still needed. In biblical times elderly people stopped working in the fields and took up their positions of honor in the city gates. This was a place of authority. Once they reached this stage in life, they were valued not for *what they did*, but for *who they were*, and for their wisdom. Today we also ought to value our seniors for what they know and who they are, and not just for what they do for others.

> When one or more of these questions remains unanswered, it can drain our emotional energy.

These major life-questions follow us through life. None of them are answered in a moment of time, or through a single word or event. We begin to assimilate answers at each stage which are reinforced throughout our lives. The Family Blessings reveal God's answers to these life-shaping questions. God intends them to be delivered to the door of our heart through the words and actions of parents, family members and whomever we give permission to speak into our lives.

When one or more of these questions remains unanswered, it can drain our emotional energy. We feel like a leaky bucket that requires constant re-filling to maintain the water level.

Also, when major events occur such as a death, divorce, or change of career, even a blessed person might need to go back and receive fresh answers to the some of these major life-questions. The woman whose spouse has suddenly left her may rightly ask, *Now that I am single again where is there a safe place for me*, or *Do I have what it takes to make it now.* She needs to be blessed in her new phase of life.

In summary, each stage of life has its own unique questions which must be answered so that blessing can be effective. The means of delivery is what we call *the three fold cord of blessing*, and that's what we will look at next.

ENDNOTE 1 The Ancient Paths, p.69, Craig Hill Author. Family Foundations Publishing, 1992.

CHAPTER 4

How Blessing Works

"This is the way you shall bless the children of Israel.
Say to them,
The Lord bless you and keep you;
The Lord make His face to shine upon you
and be gracious to you;
The Lord lift up His countenance upon you
and give you peace.
So shall they put my name on the children of Israel
and I will bless them"

Numbers 6:23-27 NKJV.

"The Ancient Hebrews recognized that words
of blessing spoken in the name of God
are somehow able to transmit the power and favor
of God"

Rolf Garborg, The Family Blessing[1]

Words, deeds and ceremonies

Many years before we understood the concepts of Family Blessing, Melissa had attempted to minister to Mary, a woman who was experiencing real emotional difficulties. The hours she spent encouraging and counseling did not have the desired effect. We lost track of her for more than 20 years until the day Mary appeared at one of our workshops. She was in better shape than when we had seen her last, but evidently still in need of a blessing. Based upon our past relationship with her, we felt the confidence and permission to deliver a spoken blessing. A few days later Mary responded;

> *...The first time you looked at me and blessed me, it went like an arrow into my heart and made me weep. So many people have asked me to give of myself over the years...So few have poured anything freely into me in return. I couldn't believe how it made me feel when you folks blessed me.*
>
> *Personally, this has had a tremendous impact on my soul. It has been water in the desert for me. I no longer just give mental consent to the fact that I am blessed in the Lord, but I actually feel it. I feel blessed! I know [I am blessed]! Hallelujah! What liberation! What immense joy! I pray that the Lord will expand your territories in sharing this powerful workshop – so many people need this!*

A few words spoken in the form of a blessing had somehow broken through to Mary's hardened heart and brought joy and new life to her soul. Why?

To comprehend the power contained in a spoken blessing we need to have a look at the astounding power inherent in words.

Words have power

Everything we see owes its existence to the power of words. Eons ago the physical world as we know it today didn't exist. Then a force was exerted that changed everything.

God spoke, and a billion stars were flung into space.

God spoke, and our solar system appeared.

God spoke, and the ball of mud we call Earth became the home for millions of exquisitely designed forms of life.

In the first chapter of Genesis more than 15 times we encounter God speaking and using words to fashion and shape every aspect of life on Earth. You could say that using the spoken word was God's *modus operandi* for creation.

Whenever the Bible records God speaking, things begin to shift, people are affected, promises are given, destinies are declared, bodies are raised from the dead, and mountains are moved. God's words have creative power and eternal nature. The prophet Isaiah declared, "The grass withers and the flowers fall, but the Word of our God stands forever" *(Isaiah 40:8 NIV).*

Words carry spiritual authority

Words permeate the spiritual atmosphere; angels sing praises and the devil spouts lies.

Through words, the devil challenged God's authority and deceived Adam and Eve.

Through words, God promised them a way of redemption.

Through words, the devil challenged God's authority and deceived Adam and Eve.

Through words, God promised them a way of redemption.

Through words, Jesus revealed the mysteries of the unseen kingdom of God and commanded a dead man to be raised.

Through words, the apostles preached the Gospel that changed the world in which they lived.

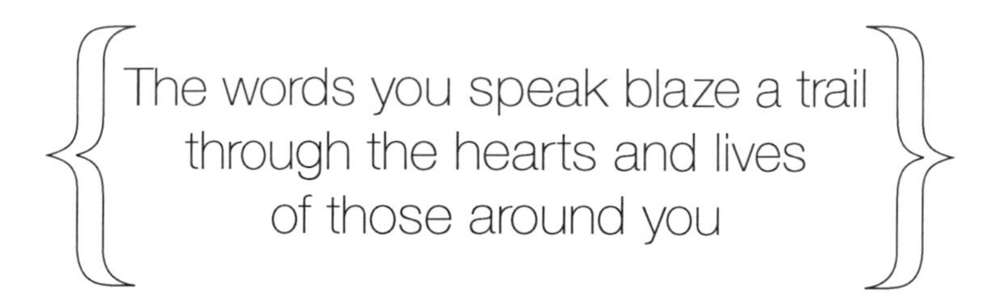

The only created beings with whom God chose to share the power of words are people. God's words gave the animals life, and Adam's words gave them an identity as he named them one by one (see Genesis 2:20).

Your words have power as well!

The Bible tells us that "death and life are in the power of the tongue" *(Proverbs 18:21).* Words you speak blaze a trail through the hearts and lives of those around you, impacting their thoughts, feelings and actions.

The most powerful words

All words are powerful. Yet some words are more powerful than others. Imagine the following scene for a moment:

The whispering ceases abruptly as the Judge re-enters the courtroom and slowly takes his seat. For two long months this room has been filled with many voices of testimony, argument, accusation and objection. But in the next moment only one voice will be heard – one that carries the full weight and authority of the law. Everyone listens intently. They understand that the words spoken will determine the future of the young woman standing before them. The judge's eyes scan the crowd, meeting briefly with the prosecutor and defense attorney, then lock onto the accused. Addressing her by name he pronounces the verdict: "*I find you NOT guilty on all charges*"

As the gavel strikes the desk, the room erupts in a mixture of cheers, tears, and sighs of relief.

Though fictional, this courtroom scene pictures a very real truth – that words have the power to change lives.

Although the judge's words are his own, when he makes a pronouncement, he speaks on behalf of the government. At that moment, his words have *legal* authority to put someone into prison or to set them free.

> the authority inherent in a spoken blessing flows from God's partnership with the words.

To pronounce blessings was one of the three main purposes of the Aaronic priesthood: "...for the Lord your God has chosen them (the priests) to minister and to pronounce blessings in the name of the Lord and to decide all cases of dispute..." *(Deuteronomy 21:5 NIV)*. The word "pronounce" carries the connotation of authority. In the same way that a judge's words represent the government that appointed him, so the priests' words of blessing carried the governmental weight of God's authority in the spiritual realm. The original language in this passage reveals that the authority inherent in a spoken blessing flows from God's partnership with the words. In Hebrew, the phrase translated "pronounce blessings" reads, *bless by their word and the Lord.* Effectively God was saying: *"If you will speak, I will act."*

God promised to partner with the priests' words to accomplish His spiritual activity in the lives of His people.

A prime example is found in the life of Aaron, the High Priest: "The Lord said to Moses, 'Tell Aaron and his sons, This is how you are to bless the Israelites. Say to them..." *(Numbers 6:22-23 NIV)*. The words that follow are called *the Aaronic blessing*. It has been used in many Christian churches for centuries.

Aaron was to bless by speaking on God's behalf. It was a corporate blessing to be given to the entire nation on a regular basis. Each time Aaron repeated these words, he stood in front of the tabernacle and faced thousands of tents containing the families of the 12 tribes of Israel. He knew that if he spoke the words of this blessing, God would infuse them with the power of His Spirit. As Aaron blessed, God was in agreement to favor the nation by protecting them from their enemies and providing for their needs. In the process, the very character of Jehovah was stamped upon the people of Israel (see Numbers 6:27).

This principle is not limited to Old Testament priests. It is a *universal principle of blessing* that we have witnessed on countless occasions. When a person speaks words of blessing, the Holy Spirit is present to write those words upon the recipient's heart just like he did for our friend Mary mentioned at the beginning of this chapter.

The three-fold cord of blessing

The power unleashed by blessing begins with words, but it does not stop there. There are three aspects that all work together" words, deeds and ceremonies. When these three elements are intentionally intertwined, they become like the three-fold cord mentioned in the Bible that cannot be broken (see Ecclesiastes 4:12).

Each strand contributes to the overall strength and permanence of the act of blessing:

Words *say* it!
Deeds *show* it!
Ceremonies *seal* it!

We have already described how the power of words is indispensable to the process. Now let's look at the dynamics involved in deeds and ceremonies.

Deeds that reinforce the blessing

The second strand in the cord is *deeds*. A deed is defined as "an intentional action that is performed, or accomplished; an exploit or achievement."[2]

Deeds make words more acceptable. Actions that agree with our words add weight and credibility to what we say. Preparing a meal to accompany a formal blessing ceremony, purchasing or making a special gift, performing an act of kindness – these are but a few among many possible deeds that demonstrate the truth of the blessing we have spoken.

One of the ways we reinforced blessing with our children was to take each one on an outing that they would enjoy. We liked to use these special events as a backdrop to speak words of blessing. For example, as soon as our daughter Jessica reached school age, Terry began to take her on "dates with Daddy." The purpose of these dates was to communicate her value as a woman.

The date usually began with Terry leaving the house and returning to pick her up in a borrowed car – usually something much nicer than our own car (preferably a convertible). After dinner and maybe a movie, mini-golf, or a walk in a park, Jessica would often share her dreams for the future. Throughout the evening Terry took every opportunity to convey respect and honor, even through little things like opening doors for her.

On the way home, Terry would give her an informal verbal blessing that concluded with words like these: "You are an extremely bright and valuable person. You are the apple of your father's eye. You were placed upon this earth by God for a great and awesome purpose. Don't ever give your heart to a man who treats you with any less *honor* or respect than I have treated you today." At that moment those words had considerably more impact than if either of us had merely spoken them around the dinner table.

Ceremonies that *seal* it

Ceremonies validate memorable moments of blessing in our lives with actions that reinforce the sincerity of the words spoken.

God commanded the Israelites to gather together several times a year and conduct ceremonies to mark special occasions. These special occasions included three feasts (see Leviticus 23). During these celebrations, work ceased and people gathered together to carry out purposeful, deliberate activities replete with symbolic gestures that reinforced their national identity and the message of

God's faithfulness. The Jewish culture today is full of time-honored ceremonies which have actually served as a bridge for the ancient blessing of Abraham still to be active today.

Our fast-paced North American culture has largely lost the connection between ceremony and celebration. For us the word *ceremony* carries the connotation of a boring ritual without much meaning. Even one of our dictionaries defines ceremony as "any formal act or observance, especially a meaningless one."

A blessing ceremony is quite the opposite. When thoughtfully planned and orchestrated, it adds a visual dimension to the process that "seals" the meaning of the spoken words. Wedding ceremonies, graduations, anniversaries, special birthdays and rites of passage, such as the beginning of teen years, are obvious times when ceremonies can help instill a blessing that lasts a lifetime. Ceremonies can form family traditions that enable the blessing to endure and grow. We will give more examples of meaningful ceremonies in later chapters.

Ceremonies do not have to be restricted to formal occasions. For example, in our family we have adopted the practice of a giving each of our adult children a New Year's blessing. Near the end of each calendar year, we ask God to speak to our hearts about Scripture passages that reflect His thoughts for each of our children for the coming year. Next, we craft words to go along with the truth to be applied to their lives. At some point we gather together in the family room. With the children seated, we begin by laying our hands on each child's head one at a time while Terry pronounces a blessing based upon what he feels God has spoken to his heart for our children. Melissa adds her words of agreement and additional insight. Terry records these blessings in his journal so that the following year we can review God's faithfulness in performing His Word in the lives of each of our family members.

Our New Year's blessing is just one variation on a theme. Families that take time to combine words of blessing creatively with deeds and ceremonies will soon find themselves forming enduring family traditions. They will discover that using a three-fold cord of words, deeds and ceremonies truly binds a family together in a healthy way.

A major event isn't always required validate a blessing. It can be sealed with a brief and informal ceremony as well. As Melissa is often heard saying, "Use any event as an opportunity to bless!"

We will never forget how a simple ceremony altered the course of one young man's life.

At a conference where we had ministered, a young man in his 20's approached us. We listened to his story and performed a simple ceremony. Among other things, the ceremony included us standing in the place of his mother and father and asking him to place all his insecurities symbolically in a box. Then we invited him to walk toward us. As he came into our arms, we spoke many things to him about his character and calling that were evident to us through personal observation and reports of his excellent reputation. He shares the impact of this celebration made:

> *In my walk with God there seemed to be something that I had not been able to attain. I felt that there was a root of some kind in my life and realized that it had to do with not having my father's blessing. For whatever reason, my father withheld his blessing from me for as long as I can remember. When I shared with my parents that God had called me into ministry, my mother was excited, but my father, because of his past, did not bless me (he had left the ministry).*
>
> *When you performed the simple ceremony of calling me forth into my adult destiny, I felt...the ground was broken to the 'new pipeline' of blessing.... It was a powerful experience.... I was able to see the moment with Jesus in the room. Jesus was the one giving me His blessing.*
> *In our culture we don't really have an occasion when a father calls his children forth and blesses them, but it is so necessary. ...Many things occurred in those moments. I have now begun a journey of discovery. For the first time in my life I am beginning to understand who I am. Since that day I have a new, conquering confidence.*

Jesus received His Father's blessing before he launched out in ministry, not after. My life is shifting from attempting to earn a blessing, to being blessed by my true Father.

When the right words are backed up by actions and even the simplest of ceremonies, the blessing becomes supernaturally effective.

We don't need to be trained counselors to bless people. The effectiveness of a blessing does not depend on our eloquence. The person who is receiving the blessing remembers the weight of God's presence far more than the eloquence of your words.

So don't be shy to begin.

You may be surprised to what extent God can use your attempt to deliver a blessing regardless of your skill level.

In the third section of this book we will guide you through a step by step process on *giving* a blessing, but before we do that, we want to take time to illustrate how the blessing works at every stage so that you can recover the blessings you have missed in preparation for giving the blessings your loved ones need.

ENDNOTE 1 Author Rolf Garborg is a dear friend – this quote comes from the original version of his book The Family Blessing. The current version is published by Summerside Press – the website is www.summersidepress.com
ENDNOTE 2_Deed. (n.d.). *Dictionary.com Unabridged (v 1.1)*. from Dictionary.com website: http://dictionary.reference.com/browse/deed.

PART TWO

Restoring the Foundations

CHAPTER 5

Why Look Back?

"Search me, O God, and know my heart. Try me and know my anxious thoughts;
And see if there be any (painful) way in me, And lead me in the everlasting way,"

Psalm 139:23-24 NASB (literal rendition).

Why do I have to look back?
Some people who attend our seminars are surprised to discover that before we teach people how to give a blessing to someone else, we spend considerable time teaching people how to recover the blessings *they themselves have missed* earlier in life. Typically, this includes a brief look back at their family of origin.

Invariably someone asks, Why do I have to look back? Can't I just forget the past?

It's an honest question. And it must be answered in a satisfactory manner before we can be effective in giving and receiving family blessings.

Here are three reasons why, at some point in your life, you must look back.

Reason #1: Denial doesn't work
Consider the extraordinary story of a soldier *who spent most of an entire century* trying to avoid the pain of his past only to change his mind at the last moment.

On August 6th 2009, thousands of people lined the streets of Somerset England to catch a glimpse of soldiers from four countries marching alongside a funeral hearse of Private Harold Patch.

A news release from the day of his funeral explains the reason for this unusual display of honor:

> "Until his death at 111 years old, Patch was the last surviving soldier to have witnessed the horrors of trench warfare in the first World War. (At nineteen years of age) Patch fought in the trenches …and was seriously wounded in Belgium in 1917 at the Battle of Passchendaele, in which 70,000 of his fellow soldiers died – including three of his close friends. He received battlefield treatment without anesthetic.
>
> "After the war, Harry (Harold) returned to his work as a plumber and later became a sanitary engineer. He married… a young girl he met while convalescing after the battle. They married in 1919 and had two sons."
>
> "*Patch didn't speak about the war until he turned 100 years old.*
>
> "He tried to suppress the memories and to live as normal a life as possible; the culture of his time said that he was fortunate to have survived and that he should get on with his life," a Ministry of Defense biography says. "That suited Harry; he could forget his 'demons' – the memories of what happened to him and to his close friends."
>
> "In 1998, a television producer with an interest in the war talked to Patch, who then made the decision to speak of his memories... He took part in a documentary on the war and began gradually to open up.
>
> "It wasn't long before Patch became a spokesman for his generation, speaking about the horrors of the war as well as his own emotions and reactions. "*In speaking about his experiences, Harry began at last to come to terms with his war, and was at peace with himself and his memories,*" the Defense Ministry said.[1]

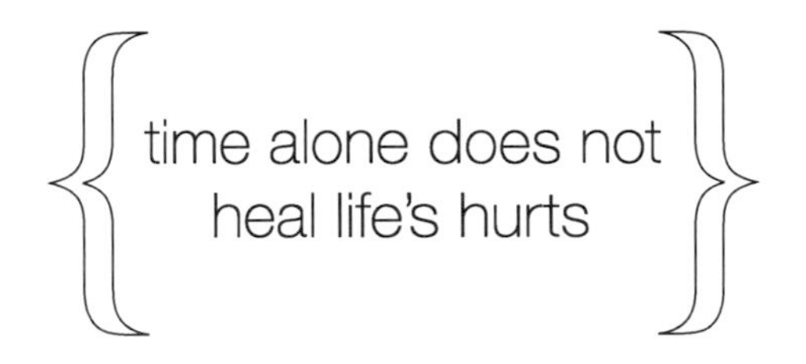

Harry tried to *suppress* his hurtful memories for more than 80 years but finally had to admit that *time alone does not heal life's hurts*. The emotional healing process he so badly needed had been "on hold" for decades. Not until Harry re-visited those memories, could the healing process begin. The results were far greater than Harry had imagined. This leads us to the second reason for looking back.

Reason #2: Pain from your past can produce power for your future.

As paradoxical as it sounds, God wants to use the most painful experiences from your past to produce the most beneficial and powerful experiences in your future. The previous news article about Harry Patch continues the story of his late life transformation:

"His thoughts then turned to reconciliation, to the long-term effects of suffering and coming to terms with that suffering. Patch returned to Belgium in 2002, *something he had said he would never do*, and laid a wreath to his battalion... Two years later, he met and shook hands with a German artilleryman from the (First World War). Patch later laid a wreath at a Cemetery for the German war dead."[2]

In 2007 Patch wrote a book, *The Last Fighting Tommy*, detailing his life. *Tommy* is a the slang term referring to British privates.

Think about it for a minute. Harry was 100 years old before he could even talk about the pain from his past. Once he began talking about it, he was eventually able to forgive and reconcile with those who injured him and killed his friends. Not only that, but his autobiography written when he was 108 years old, has become an inspiration to a whole new generation.

> It is in the area of your life where you have been emotionally wounded that God intends to give you the greatest authority and influence

Once Harry had dealt with the issues of forgiveness, he was able to convert his painful past into a powerful story to help and inspire others.

Harold Patch's story is not unlike yours. In the very area of your life where you have been emotionally wounded, God intends to give you the greatest authority and influence. Every defeat, failure and unfair circumstance in your background is fuel for God's Holy Spirit as he prepares you for your destiny. Your contribution is courage. You will need enough courage to recall your painful past in order for the process to begin.

Reason #3: You cannot give what you have not received. Countless times we have met people who believe in God's love yet remain unable to bless their families. Often the problem originates in the lies that a painful past has led them to believe about themselves and others. These lies become what we call "blessing blockers" which prevent the flow of blessing that God intends to release through family relationships.

A compelling example of this in found in the life of John, a full-time evangelist who attended a conference where we were speaking. When his mother discovered she was expecting him, his father-to-be wanted her to have an abortion. He verbally and physically abused her for allowing herself to become pregnant. When John was born he too was verbally and physically abused until his young adult years. By the time he attended our conference, John had been a Christian for more than 20 years. Although his ministry was very fruitful, none of his own adult children were serving the Lord.

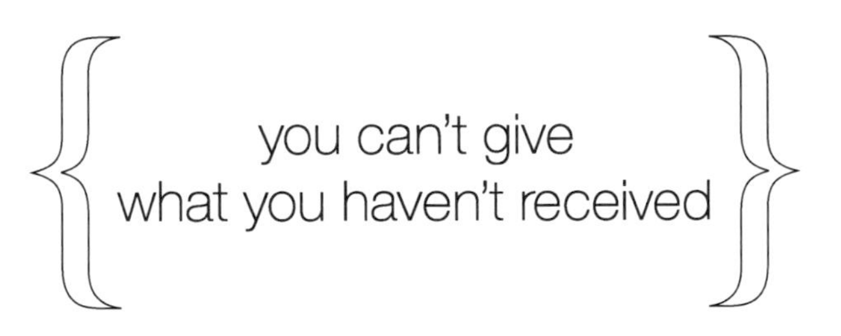

He heard about the stages of blessing, and for the first time he connected his troubled childhood with the failures he had experienced as a father. He realized that he had failed to bless his children due to the missed blessings in his own life.

During personal ministry time, John stood to receive prayer. Immediately the Holy Spirit began to take John back to memories of his abusive father. As we prayed for John, the heavenly Father spoke to him through the Holy Spirit, bringing to him the love and acceptance that was missing for so much of his life. People on the ministry team stepped in to speak the missed blessings into his life. John didn't leave it there. He also repented for his part in hating his father and contributing to the dysfunctional lifestyle in the home in which he grew up.

In the weeks following, John and his wife crafted blessings from Scripture for each of their children and spoke them aloud each day. Even though the children were not present to hear their daily confession, God heard, and He agreed with their words. One by one, the children began to resume contact with their parents who were now ready to reconcile and pass along the missed Family Blessings.

When we met them a year later, John and his wife couldn't contain the smiles as they announced that there had been significant reconciliation in the family and that all five adult children, plus two spouses, were now serving the Lord!

John discovered that *you can't give what you haven't received.* Looking back, the enemy of his soul had written part of the script for his life. John was a Christian. He had received a measure of grace and preached the gospel for a living. Part of his heart, however, was still damaged by an abusive past. Though he is a "born-again" Christian, John was still believing lies about himself and others until he received the blessings he had missed. From birth through childhood, his father's rejection had buried a lie deep within his heart that told him, You are not worthy of love. The pain lurking in his heart was the emotional equivalent to a blocked artery. It impeded the flow of blessing to his own family. After he allowed God to perform spiritual "heart surgery," the blessing flowed and his family life changed.

We cannot promise you that restoration of broken relationships will *always* occur as quickly as it did for John through spoken blessings. However, a spoken blessing will always carry spiritual power and have a positive impact on families. The process of going back to receive emotional healing and recover missed blessings will effectively *remove your past from your future.*

You will then be able to freely bless others.

It's never too late!
Your spiritual blessings are waiting in heaven's warehouse, with no expiry date attached!

Harry Patch's story is rare indeed, however we commonly see seniors receiving the blessings they have missed earlier in life. It's also never too late to pass along the blessings you failed to give to those you love.

Often parents with adult children will express deep remorse for having failed to give sufficient blessings to their children when they were raising them. During one of our seminars, a 75 year old man and his wife realized that they had not fully blessed their children.

After they had received personal ministry for their own needs, they immediately planned a family gathering to speak prepared blessings over each of their adult children and their families. They chose Thanksgiving holiday dinner as the backdrop to deliver the words that they had prayerfully crafted. We later learned that their middle-aged children were pleased and helped by this event.

In summary, removing your past from your future

We want to clarify that we are *not* advocating a life of introspection, nor are we trying to "fix" the past. Painful events from the past cannot be changed. Not all relationships can be repaired.

However the negative effects upon your heart and mind *can be repaired.* It's like hitting a severe pot hole in the road while you're driving. Later you may experience car trouble due to that event. To go back and try to fill the pothole won't help your car. The damage is under the hood. Like the pothole, a hurtful life experience remains back there, in the past, but you may still be carrying the emotional damage with you.

Be courageous and know that with the Holy Spirit's guidance you can take a brief look back at the painful event and allow God to liberate you.

Don't waste your pain! Trade it for power – the power of blessing!

You may be reading these words without being able to recall significant painful memories. In that case, please keep in mind that you do not need to be experiencing pain to have missed a Family Blessing. Even the best families "drop the ball" from time to time when it comes to instilling the blessing in children, and even perfect parents cannot protect their children from every negative influence.

As you read Part Two of this book, allow the Holy Spirit to speak to your heart concerning your personal need. The heavenly Father may have pleasant surprises in store for you.

ENDNOTE 1, 2 ibid
Last British Army WWI veteran dead at 111,
CNN.com/Europe Sunday July 26, 2009.

CHAPTER 6

Conception

Am I Welcome in this World?

"After this Elizabeth became pregnant... The Lord has done this for me," she said. "In these days He has shown His favor"

Luke 1:24-25 NIV

Your life story began before you were born.

The circumstances in which you were conceived, and how the news of your arrival was received by your parents, impacted your initial sense of welcome into this world. *Seeds of rejection can be sown at conception.* The good news is that a blessing received later in life can uproot them! This is not as mysterious as it may sound. To make it plain, here is an example of what we're talking about:

We served as Pastors of a local church for many years before we discovered the concepts of Family Blessing. During that time, a young woman named Julie contacted Terry to request pre-marital counseling.

The first appointment did not begin well. Julie kept speaking harshly to her fiancé, Shayne, and he kept trying to obtain her approval. He was oversensitive, and she didn't notice. It was awkward to watch.

Shayne was a new believer in Christ. As he shared his life story, the thought suddenly dropped into Terry's mind that Shayne may have been conceived out of wedlock and that this young man's insecurities might somehow be related to that fact. Sensing that the thought may have come from the Holy Spirit, Terry leaned toward Shayne, looked straight into his eyes and said, "Shayne, you were *not* an accident. You were meant to be on this earth." Instantly, the tension in the room dissolved as Shayne buried his head in Julie's shoulder and sobbed.

Apparently those words touched a deep need in his heart.

Shayne had indeed been a product of an unexpected pregnancy of an unmarried woman. He had also been unaccepted. The script for Shayne's identity began to be written when his mother discovered she was having the unplanned child. The words she spoke about him before his birth, and the stories she told him later, imprinted the word "accident" onto his identity.

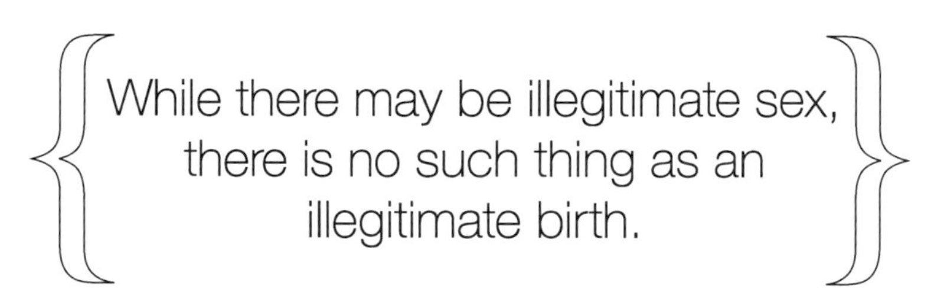

Though Shayne knew that Christ had forgiven him, he felt he did not belong. He had failed to receive the warm welcome that everyone requires at the beginning of life. Consequently at 21 years of age Shayne still believed the lie that others rejected him.

The words that Terry spoke broke that lie.

At that time we didn't know what else to say to Shayne. We simply hoped Shayne and Julie would somehow learn to love each other. If we could find Shayne today, we would add words such as these:

> *Your life didn't begin on your birthday. It began on your "earth day" – the day you were conceived. While there may be such a thing as illegitimate sex, there is no such thing as an illegitimate birth. Regardless of the circumstances of your conception, God was intimately involved on that day.*

> *Human life involves more than flesh. It requires spirit as well. Although the process is shrouded from view, when your parents' sperm and egg came together, God released spirit into the creative mix. Without the permission and involvement of heaven, you would not exist as you do today!*
>
> *The very fact that you are here today is proof that God has a plan for your life (see Psalm 139:16). In order for you to fulfill God's plan for your life, it was essential for God release you to the world when he did. He believed in you enough that He was sure you would make it through mountains of rejection and years of unanswered questions to arrive at this day. Today, all of those lies can be put to rest as you discover your unique and essential place in God's plan. We welcome you to God's world and His plan for your life.*

That's what we would *like* to have said to Shayne, and that's what we *have* said to many others because those words are true.

Some people refer to this as "blessing your spirit." Regardless of the terminology, we all need this initial welcome to fully engage in our life journey. If you have ever struggled with a sense of not belonging and a question of why you were born, or if you have sought a reason for when and where you were born, then dear one, receive the truth into the depth of your heart:
"*Welcome! You belong here!*"

We are excited that God brought you here at this time. It may even be that while you are reading these words, the Holy Spirit is adding words of truth to affirm and personalize this message to your heart. You deserve it.

Spirit, soul and body
Perhaps you are unclear about what we mean when we talk about people having a spirit, or the difference between spirit and soul. It's worth taking the time for a brief explanation:

You have a *soul*. In simple terms, your soul is your mind, will and emotions. It's the seat of your personality.

We also know that humans are uniquely gifted with a *spirit* (see 1 Thessalonians 5:23, and Hebrews 4:12). A person's spirit is *given by God* and returned to Him when the person dies (see Ecclesiastes 12:5-7).

Through our spirit we sense the presence of God, and are able to discern God's communications. Without a living spirit within us we would not be able to have a personal relationship with God through Jesus Christ.

We cannot know precisely when or how a person's spirit is made alive during the pre-birth development process. However the Bible tells us, "the life of a creature is in the blood" *(Leviticus 17:11).* We know from science that a rudimentary circulatory system becomes active within ten days after conception. It is therefore reasonable to assume that your spirit was alive within you within the first ten days.

So, we conclude that even before the announcement was made that you were on the way, you were already spiritually alive and waiting to be welcomed!

Two examples from Scripture (Luke chapter 1)

A visit with Zechariah: Zechariah, an Old Testament priest, was on duty in Jerusalem when his name was drawn by lot to minister in the Temple's Holy Place. This was a once-in-a-lifetime privilege.

While Zechariah was performing the sacred rituals alone, the angel Gabriel made a rare and unexpected appearance. He announced to Zechariah that he and his wife Elizabeth would receive the answer to their prayer of many years. Elizabeth would give birth to a son. He gave Zechariah specific details concerning the identity and destiny of their son-to-be, and told him to call him John.

"How can I be sure that what you are saying is true?" Zechariah asked the angel (Luke 1:18).

That is not what you should ask an angel who has just told you your prayers have been answered! Zechariah responded with unbelief. As a result, Gabriel applied "heavenly duct tape" to Zechariah's mouth, and he couldn't talk until his son was born.

Why did Gabriel silence Zechariah? Was it just to punish him?

The angel struck Zechariah dumb primarily to protect John!

Words are powerful – they impart blessing or cursing. By applying the angelic gag order, God prevented Zechariah from speaking wrong words about John in unbelief. If John was to be "the greatest one born of woman," as Jesus claimed, then he required the greatest blessing of anyone born. In order to ensure that John would have the fullest blessing at the first crucial stage in his life, Zechariah was rendered speechless.

He remained dumb until he was willing to give his first son an appropriate welcome in agreement with the angel's announcement of John's identity and destiny.

> The Holy Spirit is ready and willing to speak to parents about their children even at this earliest stage of life...

Nine months later, when it came time to name their little boy, a family discussion ensued. The name John, chosen by Elizabeth in response to the Angel's revelation, was against the common custom. Sons were expected to be named after their fathers. We can picture the men dismissing her so-called revelation while they discussed the reasonable options: Zechariah Jr.; Zechariah the 2nd; maybe Zach for short! Then a hush came over the group as Zechariah reached for the writing tablet upon which he scrawled authoritatively "His name is John."

At that instant, his voice returned and he burst forth in prophetic declaration of blessing upon his son. A blessing which addressed the magnitude of John's calling and God's purpose and plan for his life. The event became widely known in the region where Zechariah and Elizabeth lived. It helped affirm John's calling in the minds of many.

A visit with Mary: Meanwhile, Gabriel visited a teenager named Mary. To her he announced the prophesied virgin birth which was unprecedented and impossible without supernatural intervention.

Nevertheless, taking the angel at his word, Mary blessed the coming miraculous conception with the words, "May it be done to me, according to your word" *(Luke 1:38).* Her response was much different than Zechariah's. She responded with faith – a remarkable response in light of the shame she would have to face once word spread that she was expecting.

Zechariah, Elizabeth, Joseph and Mary – they all required angelic intervention in order to appropriately welcome their sons into the world. Without this warm welcome the unique identities of both children would have been questioned and possibly rejected.

John and Jesus had unique destinies, however every son and daughter deserves and needs *their own* unique welcome. The Holy Spirit is ready and willing to speak to parents about their children even at this earliest stage of life.

A Visit with you: Perhaps you failed to receive a warm welcome and you're thinking that it's a little too late to be looking for that blessing. Actually the heavenly Father would love to make up for that missed blessing in your life just as he did for a Pastor at one of our seminars.

Words of blessing can powerfully displace lies we might not even have recognized…

A pastor named Henry heard our teaching at a conference and realized that his life-long sense of "not belonging" had to do with the shame surrounding his arrival. His birth was the unexpected product of sexual assault. While he was a child his mother reminded him of it.

During prayer ministry one evening a picture came to his mind of a figure doing a traditional dance, jumping with excitement and crying, "That's my son!" He immediately understood Him to be God, his Father. The experience brought lasting change. Many months later Henry explained that the sense of not belonging had all but disappeared from his life:

> *"Praise God for His healing and the freedom I have. I have an identity – I'm created in the image of God, a precious son called by name before I was in my mother's womb, with a destiny. Hallelujah!"*

Henry's parents weren't available to bless him, but he received the blessing in prayer through a personal word from God while trusted friends prayed for him. When we checked with him a few years later, Henry was not only still enthused about receiving his blessing, he had now designed a brief course on Family Blessing which he was teaching to Bible college students.

Erasing and replacing a lie

Words of blessing can powerfully displace lies we might not even have recognized. Such was the case with a couple that experienced dramatic improvement in the quality of their family life through a simple act of repentance and a regular routine of speaking words of blessing. Grant and Tracy sent us this wonderful testimony:

> *Hearing your message on the response at conception, my wife and I were both convicted by the Holy Spirit. Our first two children were planned pregnancies. Yet when our third child came along she was unexpected. When my wife told me the news, I was not joyful or excited. My immediate response was, "Oh no!" because I hadn't wanted another child.*

Although I later changed my views and looked upon her as a gift of God, there has always seemed to be a response in her life, "Do I have to go to church again? I don't want to be there!" Regardless of how much we talked to her and prayed for her, this negative response persisted.... Even months before we prepared to attend a Christian camp our daughter's consistent response was, "I don't want to go, do I have to?"

We were convicted by the Holy Spirit and repented before God. The change in the last month has been incredible! Our daughter now wants to be at church. She leads in prayer, and her relationship with us is changing.

Grant and Tracy wisely understood that they needed to deal with their own heart issues before attempting to give the missed blessing to their daughter. The missing truth, "You are God's gift to us," delivered in the form of a spoken blessing, set their teenage daughter free.

It will do the same for anyone who is still missing God's warm welcome to their life journey.

CHAPTER 7

Pregnancy

Is there a safe place for me in this world?

"(Lord) you formed me in my mother's womb.
Body and soul, I am marvelously made!
You know me inside and out,
You know every bone in my body;
You know exactly how I was made, bit by bit,
how I was sculpted from nothing into something.
Like an open book, you watched me grow from
conception to birth;
all the stages of my life were spread out before you,"

Psalm 139:13-16 The Message

Can something that happened to you before you were born affect you later in life?

According to Steve, the answer is a resounding yes!

Steve and his wife Melanie served on the staff of a Bible college where we were teaching a seminar on the Family Blessings. There was a particularly strong sense of God's presence in the auditorium that day. During the session on pregnancy and birth we invited people to come forward for personal ministry.

Steve barely made it to the front before collapsing on the floor where he remained sobbing until the meeting was over. God was taking care of some deep emotional wounds.

Melanie later explained that Steve had been conceived out of wedlock by a young man and woman who led the youth group in their church. During the early days of her pregnancy, shame was the dominant emotion felt by Steve's mom. She and her boyfriend secretly traveled to the U.S. to seek an abortion. After the clinic they visited was unable to take them on short notice, they had a change of heart and resolved to keep the child. Returning home, they confessed to their family and church, both of whom readily forgave and accepted them.

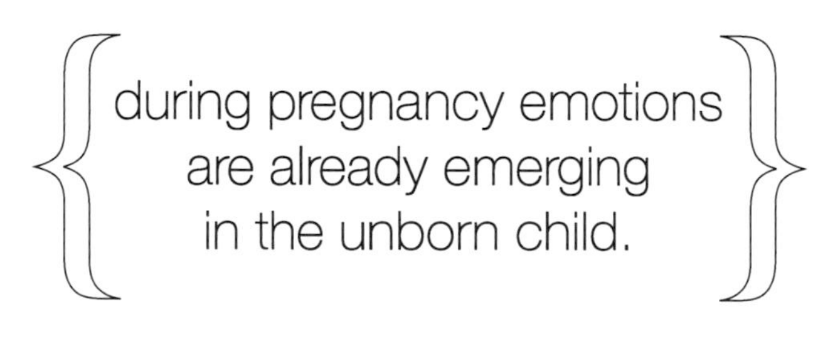

They soon married and became excited over the expected arrival. Steve's earliest memories were of a mom and dad who loved and accepted him – yet somewhere deep down he felt incomplete. He found it very difficult to share his emotions and often seemed aloof. On the day Steve heard our teaching, heaven found an inroad into Steve's heart and the Spirit spoke truth to his inner being.

The next day Melanie sent us an email describing the change in her husband:

> *Yesterday... wow! It's hard to describe what happened. All we know is that God broke that curse about his life being an "accident" and a shameful act that had to be covered. I think my husband discovered a sense of identity and belonging in Christ that he hasn't known before. I'll tell you, from a wife's perspective he is noticeably more at peace. I suppose that time will tell all that God did in him. We're still in the processing mode.*

Time did tell. Three months later Melanie added this to the story:

> *I can definitely say that the results have lasted. My husband is softer now. He has a greater servant's heart. His relationship with his parents is growing deeper than it has ever been, and he is consistently making time to be with them. The work that God did in my husband also seemed to give him more of a pastor's heart for the people to whom we minister. The best way to describe the lasting change is to call it "softness" – praise God!*

"Fearfully and wonderfully made"

Stories like Steve and Melanie's should not take us by surprise when we come to realize that during pregnancy emotions are already emerging in the unborn child.

King David described his pre-born days using the phrases, "I was fearfully and wonderfully made" (*KJV*), or as *The Message* version of Psalm 139 puts it, "Body and soul I am marvelously made." Ultrasound images show only a small segment of this multi-faceted development process.

As soon as heaven gave permission for your life journey to begin, your parents, *especially your mother*, were assigned as the gatekeepers of your tiny unprotected spirit embedded in the womb. Even before you were fully formed and ready to greet the external world, the methodical formation of your body included a mind with an increasing ability to think and feel.

It is common knowledge that whatever an expectant mother permits into her body will be passed on in measure to her child's body. Research has also confirmed that the same can be true for emotions. A substantial body of evidence gleaned from many sources indicates that pre-born children readily absorb their mother's stress. With no way of knowing what to accept and what to reject, they are totally dependent upon the protection of the one who is carrying them inside their own body.

Fortunately we can also absorb positive emotions, as we see in the example of the two pre-born boys, Jesus and John the Baptist. Blessing reached them before they were born through the interplay between their mothers, Mary and her older female relative Elizabeth.

Two expectant mothers that needed a blessing

The stories of Mary and Elizabeth and their first-born children were recorded by Dr. Luke (see Luke 1:26-56) who always had a special place for women in his writings, and perhaps even delivered a few babies in his day.

Mary, a young, newly pregnant, unmarried girl needed a blessing. She needed it quickly!

Scripture does not speak of how her own immediate family received the news. However, it is certain that her hometown of Nazareth would have been filled with gossip about the event. Who would have believed that she was carrying the Lord of the universe within her?

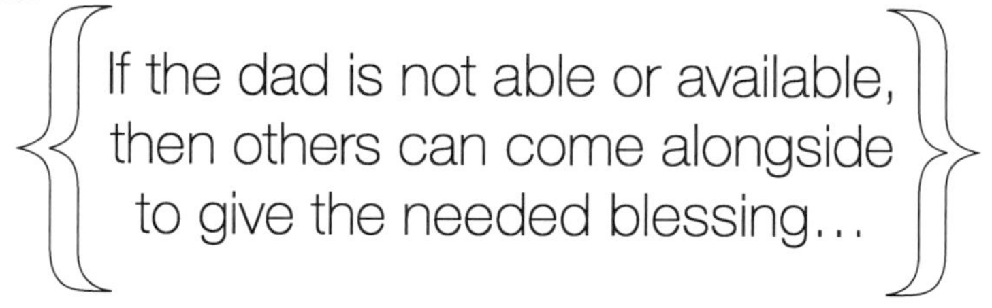

But God had prepared a safe place for Mary and the unborn Jesus during her crucial first trimester – the home of her friend and extended family member Elizabeth. Before Mary and her tiny Little One could hear any negative words of shame or cursing, she hurried to visit with her older mentor. When Elizabeth heard Mary's greeting, her own pre-born son, John, *leapt* in her womb. They were both filled with the Holy Spirit and Elizabeth spoke a powerfully prophetic blessing over Mary and her baby:

"Blessed are you among women, and blessed is the child you will bear. Blessed is she who has believed that what the Lord has said to her will be accomplished" *(Luke 1:42, 45).*

Elizabeth was the first person in history to recognize Jesus as her Lord. She acknowledged Him as being fully God and fully man even while He was still inside His mother.

Elizabeth was favored; Mary was blessed. Mary's famous prophetic poem of blessing, the *Magnificat,* is recorded for all of history to read and sing. She was truly a blessed woman, and all generations have called her blessed (see Luke 1:48).

Mary, just like many moms, was in a position for major stress during her pregnancy. She found a safe place with a trusted friend who stood in for the absent relatives to give the needed blessing. May her story provide this source of encouragement:

If the dad is not able or available, then others can come alongside to help create a safe environment and give the needed blessing!

We encourage single moms to speak the heavenly Father's blessing prophetically into the lives of their pre-born children *even if the men are absent!*

A woman's perspective
In addition to being a professional Doula (labor and delivery coach), Melissa has also spent many informal hours speaking into the lives of expectant moms. In her own words:

> *Pregnancy! What a blessing and privilege! As a mother of three children, I can say, what an honor it is to have been a co-creator with God. I have borne three eternal souls, created in His image, for His glory, because He wanted them here on earth. Thank you Lord!*
>
> *I believe that pregnant women are to be honored with special treatment – the "red carpet" should be rolled out for them.*
>
> *What is happening in their bodies for nine months is miraculous and holy. The Holy Spirit is brooding over them the way He brooded over Mary so long ago. The Lord is with them as He was with Mary. They are favored, having the amazing responsibility and stewardship of another life within them.*

For this reason, in our ministry I have taken a special interest in every pregnant woman I encounter. Somehow I can "sniff" them out in a room even before they are "showing. I asked once where we ministered, 'Is anyone here expecting?' The woman I asked had found out that she was pregnant just that day. Like a magnet, I am drawn to them because they need a blessing.

Women in the middle years, the Elizabeth years, have a special calling to bless young Marys whom God brings their way. Thus I have made it a purpose in life to bless new life from conception to birth. I have prayed with many, many women through their nausea-filled first trimesters, through the sometimes tedious second trimester, and the uncomfortable, hope-filled third trimester, to full term. We have prayed together through labor and delivery, in good times – full-term, healthy births, and hard times – miscarriages, traumatic births, developmentally delayed babies and single-parent pregnancies, to name a few. Each baby needs a blessing regardless of circumstances. The baby needs to feel, yes, it is a safe place, and there are people who love me and welcome me into the world. On many occasions I have felt babies move vigorously in the womb as the blessing is spoken.

On a side note, it has also happened on several occasions, that after blessing a married woman who has not been able to conceive, within a year we receive the photo of her first child!

The blessing can increase when the generations work together. A conference where we ministered was held in the central town of a farming community. In attendance was a young, expectant woman whose father was also present. After teaching on the nature of blessing, we spoke words of blessing to both the mother and child. Then we invited the grandfather of the child, the mother's dad, to add his words.

Tears streamed down the lined face of that farmer as he struggled to express what he desired for this child. We will never forget the loud amens that rang through the room as he closed with these words: "And may you be saved from having to experience the troubles that our generation went through."

Whatever those troubles may have been, the people from the community understood what he meant, and those words released faith in the room. They affected everyone who knew the family. They were "weighty" and carried spiritual significance.

Just as Aaron the high priest's words of blessing released the power of God upon the ancient children of Israel, so these sincere words spoken by the grandfather will positively affect the child and her mother, for life.

CHAPTER 8

Birth

Will my needs be met in this world?

"The child's father and mother marveled at what was said about Him. Then Simeon blessed them and said... 'This child is destined...'

Luke 2:34

"This child is destined..."

What impressive words! What authority in his voice!

Who was this old man and what right did he have to make such a confident assertion to young Mary and Joseph about their infant son Jesus?

By the time Simeon spoke these words of blessing over Jesus, Joseph and Mary could hardly keep track of all the wonderful things being said about their child. What started as an untimely delivery in a stable, had transformed into the most memorable month of their lives for the best of reasons.

Luke's gospel provides us with a pattern for blessing any child at birth

Jesus and His earthly parents had been blessed more than anyone had anticipated. On more than one occasion perfect strangers had spoken to them about their child's identity and God's destiny for His life. It was no longer a secret. The word was "out there" that this child had a very special future.

You might think, Of course there were prophecies and blessings spoken over Jesus when He was born. After all He is the Savior of the world! True enough. The uniqueness of Jesus is clearly demonstrated in what was said about Him at birth. No other person will ever receive words such as those spoken to Mary and Joseph.

On the other hand, this narrative from Luke's gospel provides us with *a pattern for blessing any child at birth.* Before we examine this pattern in greater detail, let's first review the questions addressed by Family Blessing at this early stage of life.

What is the blessing needed during infancy?

At the moment a baby is born, all five senses are active, and billions of cells within a child's brain are processing the input. The question, Will my needs be met? is beginning to be addressed in the newborn's first hours through the way the child is touched, held, fed and spoken to.

Before learning his/her parents' language, a child feels the emotional needs for belonging and acceptance. Through experience the child learns how these needs are met.

Thus the warm welcome that the little one received prior to birth is now reinforced through "hands-on" activities of the mother and dad. As a child develops from infant to toddler, responses to the first three major life-questions continue to be reinforced:

Am I welcome?
Where is there a safe place for me?
Will my needs be met?

These are questions of *belonging.* They are foundational for emotional stability later in life. Teens or adults plagued by feelings of insecurity and anxiety may discover that the roots of these feelings lead directly back to this early period of life. On this point science and Scripture agree – what happened to you during *your pre-born days and period of infancy can impact your pattern of thought and feelings even as an adult.*

The good news is always the same – missed blessings can be recovered at any point in your life. Before we say any more about that, let's first return to the story of Jesus' birth to discover how the heavenly Father used some unusual circumstances to ensure that His Son received sufficient Family Blessing as a newborn child.

Can't you wait to get back home?

Out on the road with no accommodation, friends or family – can you imagine worse timing for a young woman to have her first child? Back home in Nazareth mid-wives and family were preparing for this event. But Mary had to give birth without their help. With every local Inn fully booked, Joseph and Mary were stuck in a stable. It was probably a stone cave where animals slept.

In those days women sometimes died during childbirth. Caesarean sections were not an option. While lying on the straw in a dimly lit cave in the final stages of labor, Mary was not singing the *Magnificat!* And in the first moments after delivery, the joy of seeing their firstborn must have been dampened by the fact that none of the family was present to share it.

Fortunately, God had anticipated the need. Shepherds arrived in response to an angelic announcement. Mary and Joseph must have been in awe when the shepherds told them what they had seen. The shepherds' timely visit would have mitigated the harshness of the situation. Their words spiritually strengthened everyone present.

In the biblical story, the shepherds added to the blessing by taking care of the birth announcement. According to Luke, after they had seen Jesus they told everyone what the angels had said about His identity. Thus Jesus' true identity was already being spread throughout the community!

Why Bethlehem?

Some may hear this explanation and still wonder, Weren't there shepherds in Nazareth as well? Why did God lead Mary and Joseph so far from home?

If Jesus had been born in Nazareth, Mary may have had a less traumatic delivery, but Jesus may have received the "wrong" blessing. It is evident in later years of Jesus' life that extended family members didn't understand who He was. Many didn't accept His identity until after His resurrection. It's easy to imagine a family member picking Him up a few hours after birth and exclaiming, Doesn't He look just like His father Joseph!

> God brought people, unrelated to the family, alongside Mary and Joseph when they needed a blessing.

Just like Mary needed to be away during part of her pregnancy, perhaps God knew she needed to be away at the time of delivery. The angelic birth announcement might not have been as readily received in Nazareth as it was by those who weren't related to Jesus.

Today labor and delivery are also crucial times when family and friends can bring great comfort and blessing. We will never forget the support of our church family during the labor and delivery of our firstborn child. Twenty hours into the labor Terry was on the phone to a friend who had promised to "pray us through." As they agreed in prayer, our son David began the last stage of his journey from darkness to light.

Since then Melissa has felt called to commit herself not only to pray for mothers during labor, but to work with them as a coach during pregnancy. Sometimes after the doctor delivers the baby Melissa immediately delivers a blessing.

Why is ceremony important?

Blessings intended at birth go beyond the immediate family. When a child is born, he or she is to be officially welcomed into the community of faith and placed under the umbrella of God's protection through the prayers of those in spiritual authority.

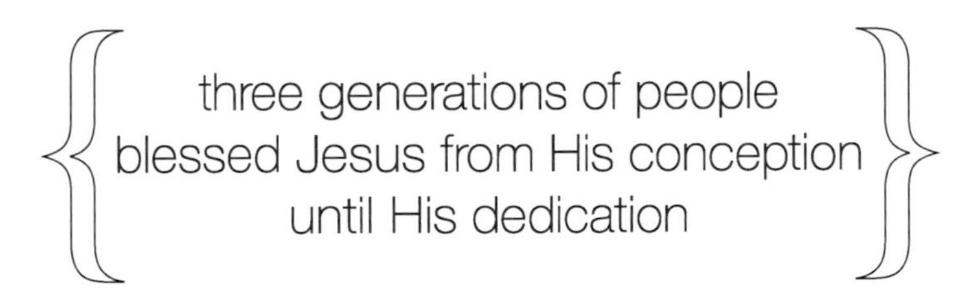

About a month after the birth of their Son, Mary and Joseph returned with Jesus, and probably several family members, to the temple in Jerusalem to observe the mandatory dedication ceremony carried out by priests. Once again God brought people, unrelated to the family, alongside them when they needed a blessing.

God had spent years preparing two senior saints to speak with insight from the Lord concerning Jesus' identity and destiny. It was something Mary, Joseph, or the priests apparently would not have been able to do on their own. Simeon was "moved by the Spirit" to be at the right place at the right time. Gently picking up the baby in his arms, he announced Jesus' destiny and blessed Mary and Joseph, encouraging them in their new role as parents.

Then an old saint who had spent her life serving God through prayer in the temple, stepped forward and revealed what God had spoken to her about this child. Anna completed the blessing that the Father in heaven had prepared for His only Son at His birth.

Now three generations of people had blessed Jesus from His conception to His dedication: Mary the young mother; the middle-aged family relative Elizabeth; and Simeon and Anna, the senior saints.

How does ceremony work today?
A dedication ceremony ought to be more than a ritual. God intends for it to have spiritual impact upon the child and the family.

The welcoming of a new child into the community of faith is a joint celebration between heaven and earth. It's a time when God can empower the family with treasures from His storehouse to equip them to guide their child into his or her destiny. Whether your church practices infant baptism or a dedication ceremony, imparting blessing is the order of the day.

When we served as pastors, we made a *big* deal out of baby dedications in our Sunday services. We often invited both sets of grandparents, relatives, god-parents, and friends whom the parents choose, to stand alongside the family. We urged parents to choose a life-Scripture to publicly proclaim over their child. We announced the meaning of the child's name, and invoked special prayers that included time for seeking the guidance of the Holy Spirit concerning the child's destiny.

Sometimes God gave insights about the child's future through prophetic words at that very moment. When that happened, we would encourage parents to record them and allow the truth of the words to be tested over time.

The power of the Holy Spirit
Even though our dedication ceremonies were well planned in advance, on occasion we were surprised by the Holy Spirit's agenda revealed during the dedication itself.

During one particularly large ceremony, family and friends of the parents lined the front of the sanctuary from one side of the room to the other. We shared the truth that God is the author of the life of every child who is conceived, a first-time visitor in the church, a single mother, received profound insight. It set her free from shame and opened to doorway to blessing. Here is her story:

> *I was raised in a Christian home, but had been away from both God and church for more than ten years. I found myself*

in a new town, unemployed, alone and pregnant with my third child. Feeling desperate, I attended a morning service while a baby was being dedicated. I couldn't help feeling so alone and full of shame.

Pastor Terry, whom I had never met, said that God had just put something on his heart to share. He said that God wanted somebody to know that every child is a gift from Him, and that no matter what the circumstance, each child was created for a reason. I knew that was meant for me, and felt instantly touched by God's love. God opened my eyes to see how much He loved me and my children. "[I now attend] a home fellowship group led by the parents of the baby that was dedicated at that morning service where God spoke to me.

It was thrilling to see a single mother find new friends and learn to bless her own child by watching the blessing and dedication of another couple's baby.

The predictions of the Holy Spirit

Spirit-led words of blessing spoken at the time of a child's dedication can become a powerful influence in shaping a child's future. This is demonstrated in the life of a friend of ours named Steve who has this to say:

> *I am the oldest of six children. My parents met as single missionaries in Malawi, Africa. Shortly after my brother was born, our parents decided to dedicate us as part of the African church tradition. I know that my parents did not understand the power of blessing as we do now. Neither would they have believed at that time in the gift of prophecy, but they did love God and were led by the Spirit as they knew how. As part of our dedication, they blessed us both to become full-time Christian workers.*
>
> *They never told this to me or my brother as we were growing up. In fact whatever career we talked about, they endorsed. My brother and I however, both pursued Bible college training and we both became pastors. It was only then that our parents told us of the blessing they had prayed over us.*
>
> *Of interest to me is that my parents did not pray a similar blessing over any of our other siblings and while most are active followers of Jesus, only my brother and I are in full-time ministry.*

We had a similar experience with our third child Mark.

A woman in our church at the time gave us a life-shaping Scripture for Mark when he was born. Along with the Scripture she shared what she felt the Holy Spirit was saying about our boy's future. We pondered her words, and like Mary, treasured them, holding them close to our hearts for more than a dozen years.

One day when our son was 13, he felt God speak something similar to his heart. Only then did we decide to share those words with him. Today we have already seen some of the words spoken about Mark come to pass, and we are able to help him plan for the special future that is slowly unfolding in his life.

What's in a name?
Names are inextricably bound to a person's identity. The name a child is given is to be part of his/her blessing at birth.

Bible names were generally assigned for their meaning and purpose. For example, Joseph had the right and responsibility to name Mary's Son. He followed the angel's instructions to name Him Jesus – meaning, "The Lord Saves." A name was officially conferred on a child at circumcision. From the day of Jesus' circumcision onward, every time someone spoke His name, they prophesied His future.

The name you have been given may not seem meaningful, yet we are constantly surprised at how God can reveal His purpose and meaning through an apparently arbitrary choice. We devote an entire chapter on name blessings in the third section of this book to delve into this further.

For people like Steve and Mark, stamped into their being is the understanding that they were desired by their parents, prepared by God beforehand, welcomed when they arrived, and gifted uniquely for a life-purpose in God. They know the meaning of their names and how they reflect their calling in life. Their birth stories are a source of blessing to them. *That's what God intends for every child!*

If, however, your life-story leaves you aching for that sense of significance and security, then rest assured that the heavenly Father still has every one of your missed blessings stored up in heaven's warehouse waiting to be delivered.

Ask Him to erase and replace the lies you have believed about who you are and why you arrived on earth.

Ask Him to reveal his plan for delivering your early life-blessings.

Then watch carefully for He is sure to begin to bring an "Anna" or "Simeon" your way to release words of destiny into your life.

CHAPTER 9

Early Childhood

Major life question: Who Can I trust in this world?

"To ensure a blessing is fully received, a person needs five positive messages for every one negative message spoken to them"

Alf Davis

"Little Children have BIG feelings"

Anonymous

Early childhood, from pre-school to pre-teen age, is the period of life in which long term memories are first formed. Contained inside those memories are important scenes and words that help shape what we believe about ourselves, others and even God.

A friend of ours was praising his young child for some small accomplishment. His mother, who happened to be visiting at the time, interrupted him to say, "You compliment your children too much. You're going to make them proud." He shrugged his shoulders when telling us this story, and shared how harsh his own childhood had been. Like so many other childhoods we have heard about, his was characterized by too little affection and too much correction.

“as the twig is bent, so grows the tree!”

Where did we get the misconception that character in little people is built through constant correction? The truth is that *being corrected without being affirmed produces a feeling of rejection*. It curses rather than blesses.

Yes, discipline is essential, and we will address it, but let’s understand that a parent’s first role in a child’s life is to provide and protect, not punish and correct.

Kind words nourish little souls like plant food on tender shoots. Critical words bend and even break them. A wise man once said, “as the twig is bent, so grows the tree!” We have seen far too many “bent twigs” grow up to be bent right-out-of-shape “trees.” In fact, the way some people dishonor children makes us downright angry. We are in good company on that score, for even Jesus became angry about the treatment of little lives He desired to bless.

Jesus – blessing the toddlers

“People were bringing little children to Jesus to have Him touch them… and He took the children in His arms, put His hands on them and blessed them,” *(Mark 10:13a, 16 NIV).*

Parents brought their small children to Jesus for Him to bless them. They believed that God’s favor would be upon every little life that received loving words and a meaningful touch from the Master’s hands.

The wording for *little ones* in the original language refers to young children (*paidion* in Greek), not babies. Most were likely at that marvelous stage of life where trust comes naturally and social graces have not yet been learned. It’s easy to picture Jesus picking up one of them to pray for them while the others clamor about Him crying,

Me too!

The disciples criticized the people for "bothering" Jesus with little children. You can almost hear them saying, Take that kid out of here! She's getting in the way! Don't you know that the Master is preparing to give an important message from God?

Yes, He was about to give an important message from God – *to the disciples.* In Mark's gospel it says that Jesus became "indignant." This word means to be angry over injustice. Jesus looked the disciples square in the face and rebuked the rebukers saying, "Let the little children come to me and do not hinder them." The words had impact. Jesus made it plain that a person's value is not determined by their age or abilities. The blessing He gave them imparted spiritual life, invited God's favor, and set an example for parents to follow.

Jesus – blessed as a toddler

Push the "rewind button" for a moment and we find that Jesus was also blessed when He was a toddler. We are referring to the familiar story of the visit from the wise men. The traditional Christmas card version of this story doesn't quite line up with Scripture (*There weren't three kings riding on a one-humped camel suddenly appearing beside the manger on the night of Jesus' birth!*)

Matthew's gospel tells us that they were *Magi,* men of high social standing from a land to the east. They had seen a sign in the heavens which they interpreted as an indication of the birth of a king. Upon arriving in Jerusalem they sought and found "the young child." The word used here in reference to Jesus is the same word used in reference to the children Jesus blessed. The Savior of mankind was no older than pre-school age when the Magi blessed Him, yet these important men gave Him honor reserved for a king. They were not embarrassed to kneel before Him and worship Him.

Obviously the actions of the Maji were uniquely applicable to Jesus, however both Matthew chapter two and Mark chapter ten reveal that honor can not only be given by the younger to the older generation, but also from the older to the younger. Showing appropriate honor does not "spoil" a child. Rather it provides a nourishing environment whereby Family Blessing can be given. Unfortunately, that doesn't always happen.

Little people have *big* feelings. And when their feelings are discounted by adults, that creates dishonor that blocks the needed blessing. Here are some of the common ways in which parents dishonor their children and block the blessing that God intends.

Improper punishment: Dr. James Dobson says that the will of a child emerges in the first year and dominates by the second. Somewhere during the second year of children's lives they discover that they are independent entities that can walk anywhere they choose and put anything in their mouth light enough to pick up with their own hands.

They experiment with their newfound physical freedom without the benefit of any life experience –a recipe for disaster if left unchecked. That's why during this time period the word many children hear more than any other is *No!*

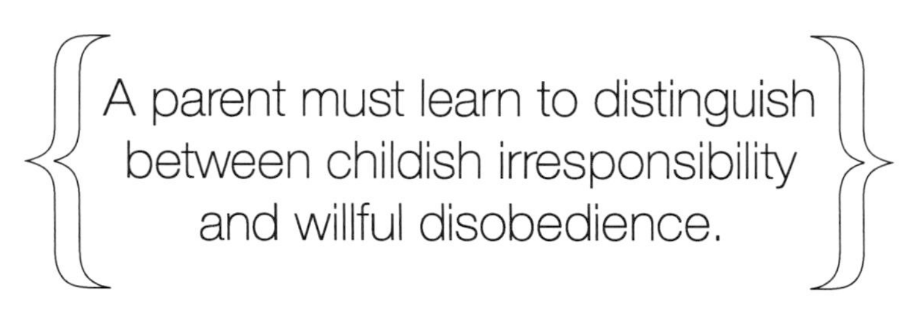

The challenge for parents at this stage is to "shape the will" without "breaking the spirit". Parents need to apply wise and balanced love and limits to bring proper correction without damaging a tender young personality.

Children become "bent out-of-shape" when parents mistake punishment for discipline.

Punishment is pain administered as a form of payment for wrongdoing, whether physical, or in the form of temporary denial of privileges.

Discipline, on the other hand, is the training of the will to make godly choices.

The goal of parental discipline is to bring children to the place where they have enough inner motivation to make good choices on their own.

Punishment accomplishes the desired discipline *only* when it is administered *in the correct circumstances* and the *correct conditions.*

A parent must learn to distinguish between childish irresponsibility and willful disobedience. A child may leave the water faucet running – that's likely just childish irresponsibility. But when a child knows what is right to do, has the ability to do it, and still chooses to do the wrong thing – *that's willful disobedience.* Punishment must only be administered when there is deliberate and willful disobedience, not childish irresponsibility.

Yet even when reserved for occasions of willful disobedience, punishment may not accomplish the goal unless it is administered in the following manner:

- it must "fit the crime" (tailored to suit the situation and the child's personality)
- be given without anger
- never be administered before the child has been warned
- be consistent from one occasion to another

The application of godly discipline must be tailored to each child. You must discover what motivates the child before you can assist in training their will. Children who have been punished unfairly receive confusing and hurtful messages about their own value and worth. They often harbor deep resentment that remains buried until it bursts forth later in life.

Another form of improper punishment is neglect. The old saying that "two wrongs don't make a right" is applicable here. *By neglecting to spend the time and effort to administer proper punishment, a parent unwittingly encourages rebellion.*

Sexual experiences: A child's trust in the early years can be decimated by sexual abuse.

Sexual abuse is one of the greatest breaches of trust that a child can experience. It not only blocks blessing, it curses a child's sense of identity, and is, unfortunately, far more common than we want to admit. If you were sexually abused as a child, then please understand that the child victim of an adult aggressor is never at fault. You did nothing to deserve such dishonor, but you must do something about the wound.

Time on its own does not heal this kind of wound. Our advice to you is this: start the process of rebuilding trust by speaking with a qualified professional who shares your spiritual values.

School experiences: Teachers are tremendously influential in shaping children's self worth at the elementary school level.

Most of us can remember a moment of shame or embarrassment at the hands of an insensitive teacher.

On the other hand, a teacher who believes in a student and recognizes their gifting can instill worth and value when it is missing in a child's life. A man at one of our workshops testified that he was never affirmed in his family and was subject to much criticism at a young age. However, one of his school teachers believed in him and made a habit of speaking encouragement into his life in such a way that this man began to believe in his own potential. Today he credits the teacher for single-handedly bestowing on him blessing that was so lacking in his life. God bless teachers who bless!

Accidental injury: Sometimes the worst injuries are the ones that happen accidentally. Ice hockey, for example, is known to be a rough sport – body contact is permitted and encouraged. When Terry played, no one feared his body checks, because they didn't hurt. But on one occasion Terry accidentally fell onto another player while chasing a loose puck. The poor fellow had to be carried off the ice on a stretcher – and he didn't walk again for six weeks. Accidents happen and they hurt!

Accidental emotional injuries happen too, and they hurt as well. Not only that, they can block blessing from reaching a young child as effectively as deliberate mistreatment.

At a missionary conference where Terry was speaking, a married couple sought personal counsel for this very reason. They were deemed successful, and were well liked, yet the wife Brenda suffered silently. She had heard from her mother many times how painful she had been to deliver at birth. "See – you're the cause of all my pain," the mother often said in jest, *all the time thinking that Brenda understood she was just being teased.* But Brenda took it seriously. She harbored the lie and carried it into adulthood where it "bent" her relationship patterns. In her own words:

> *I have walked with the Lord for 30 years, and from the first day I was convinced of God's amazing love for His children. However, I struggled to believe that He loved me. Inwardly I suffered with a spirit of rejection. I had two loving parents, a great family and good friends, yet I couldn't break free from self-condemnation and self-hatred.*
>
> *After the family blessing teaching…the Lord revealed a number of issues…and showed Himself in each step of my life from the very beginning. Something was supernaturally unlocked for me. Since that time I have experienced an ability to accept myself (both strengths and weaknesses), I have less fear of people, and a new understanding of God's limitless love for me. …My ministry on the mission field has been enhanced and my relationships are deeper.*

Later that year some of Brenda's friends told us that they had noticed a positive and permanent change in her behavior.

Harmful vows: Children who are dishonored in any of the ways which we have described may appear to be unaffected on the outside for a period of time, but on the inside they are affected deeply. They become prone to making false conclusions about life, and this can lead them into making harmful vows.

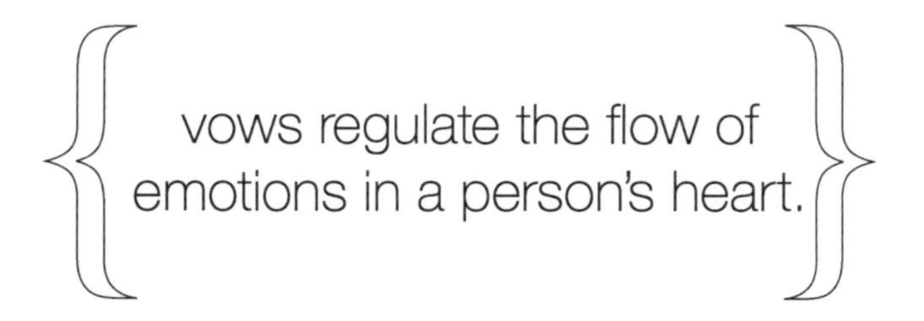

Vows are like valves. Our home has valves on the water pipes that enable us to close off the water supply to a portion of the house temporarily while a leaky faucet is being fixed. No matter how great the water supply, you don't get the flow back until the valve is re-opened.

Similarly, vows regulate the flow of emotions in a person's heart. Vows can be helpful or harmful, depending on whether they are used to open or close our heart. A marriage vow is helpful because it serves as a constant reminder to open our heart to our spouse in times when there's barely a trickle of love flowing. On the other hand, some vows shut off the supply of love and blessing.

Once children are old enough to discover and use willpower to get what they want, they can also use willpower to compensate for emotional injury. That's a vow. In an attempt to avoid more hurt, they make a vow with an act of their will. Blessing cannot flow to the part of the heart that is being protected by a vow. The same act that shuts out hurt, also keeps out love.

For example, let's say that dad promises to take his son Brent fishing on Saturday. Brent counts the days, daydreaming about the big fish that will be his. Saturday morning comes and Brent is sitting on the front step waiting. Dad walks by with his briefcase on the way to a meeting he had forgotten about when he promised the fishing expedition. He tries to cover his mistake with a promise of an "even better trip" next week. But next week, dad is out of town, and by next month he has forgotten his promise. The fishing trip never happens. Through this event Brent begins to believe a lie – perhaps that he is not worth much, or that adults cannot be trusted. He may decide he will "never trust an adult again." That part of Brent's heart is shut off.

Other similar vows include:

- I will never let anyone love me.
- I will never share what is mine.
- I will never let anyone know I am hurt.
- I will never allow anyone to touch me.

Many other statements can become vows as well, but they all have the same effect. Time does not heal a vow even when it has been temporarily forgotten. A vow must be recognized and renounced. When that happens, the lie associated with the vow can be instantly replaced with truth.

Let's get started

In this chapter, we have focused on the things that can block the needed blessings. In the third section of this book, we give specific instructions on how to give a spoken or written blessing for children and adults. Everything is there to help you get started, including the five elements that are common to any blessing.

In addition to formal occasions and special events, every parent can take a couple of simple steps to begin to incorporate words of blessing into daily family life.

A few unhurried minutes spent with a child one on one just before bed time – perhaps the most teachable time in their day – can have a huge impact. A bed time story and a little talk about how special the child is to mom and dad, followed by a hug and a prayer, may take two minutes, but it gives the gift of meaningful touch and a spoken message, and it communicates a high value on the relationship.

Our friend and author Rolf Garborg spoke the Aaronic blessing over his children every night before they went to sleep for more than a dozen years. After speaking those familiar sentences he would add his own special words according to the need of the moment. Consistency is demonstrated in active commitment. Rolf's daughter became so attached to the blessing he spoke over her each night, that before he left on business trips, she insisted he speak the blessing over her once for each day he would be away! The sense of importance, value and worth that was communicated to his children has never left them. Today Rolf's adult children continue this same practice with their own children. The family will likely continue the tradition for many generations to come.

Family dinners, or even better a family Sabbath evening, provide excellent opportunities to speak verbal blessings.

We helped our children picture a special future by praying with them about their future spouses when they were still pre-teens. Terry talked to our daughter Jessica about the special man she hadn't yet met, but whom God was even then preparing for her.

Melissa told our boys how one day they would meet the girl that God had picked out just for them. We constantly spoke of the good things that God prepares for those who obey Him. These often repeated blessings created an environment in which God was given permission to become intricately involved in the life choices of each of our children. Many years have passed since we began to bless our children in this way. As young adults, each one has experienced God's guidance in the search for a life mate and God's favor upon their life calling.

Be creative! The appendices in the back of this book give instructions, format and sample blessings for the ones you love.

Be bold! Be willing to permit God's Spirit to heal the wounds of your past in order to remove every blockage to the flow of blessing to and from your life.

CHAPTER 10

Teen Years

Do I have what it Takes?

"And Jesus kept increasing in wisdom and stature and in favor with God and men"

Luke 2:52 NIV

"My Father gave me the greatest gift anyone could give another person: he believed in me"

Jim Valvano[1]

"You can do it!"

Our son Mark was in a close foot race with several competitors as they sprinted up a long, steep hill in a regional cross-country event.

"You're looking strong, Don't let up!"

Terry could see that Mark was not yet winded. As he rounded the top, dad ran beside him for a few yards, calling out to him, "*Now's the time to make your move. See you at the finish line!*"

From the beginning of the race Terry had been positioning himself at points along the way shouting words of encouragement and strategy he had derived from running that exact route 30 years before. After taking a shortcut down the hill, dad hopped a fence and waited on the track to witness his son's finishing kick in the final yards of the race.

"Great finish! Amazing run!"

Competing against boys up to two years older than himself, Mark still managed to finish in the top 60 out of a field of 400 runners. Although this invitational didn't count toward school rankings, *the race certainly counted in the young man's heart*. He began to believe that he really did have what it takes.

Before the race Mark had a different opinion. With an exceptional athlete as a running mate, and being prone to self-criticism, Mark had developed an inaccurate view of his own abilities. He felt he could never measure up. After many attempts around the kitchen table, we still couldn't talk our son out of this misconception. Terry decided to try to "be there" and shout words of affirmation at key moments during an actual race. It worked.

Mark's race is a metaphor for adolescence. It's so easy for young minds and hearts to receive the wrong message during this crucial stage of development.

At puberty, a child's body suddenly begins to mature, becoming fully adult in a very short period of time. This physical process triggers a crucial question of the heart: Do I have what it takes to make it in an adult world?

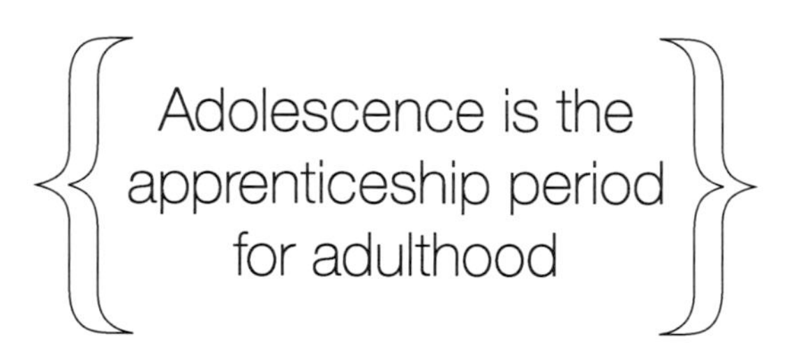

Regardless of how well a teen develops physically, this major life-question *must* receive a satisfying answer before a young person can fully embrace their emerging adult identity. This is a time period when a whole new set of fears can take hold in the heart and therefore the need for affirmation increases.

It is also a crucial time for parents. Adolescence is the apprenticeship period for adulthood.

The shift is on!

There are two significant shifts that need to happen during this apprenticeship period in order to sufficiently prepare a child for his or her adult identity.

First, *the leading role in imparting the blessing shifts from Mother to Father*.

Don't misunderstand this statement. Mothers and fathers are both important at every stage. However God has designed mothers to be the "nest builders." Typically they love to create a safe environment in which to nurture their young children. They instinctively take the lead in this regard. However there comes a time when every little bird needs to become more independent and fly from the nest.

Impartation of the Family Blessing at this stage of life becomes essential in the delivery of the required elements for balanced growth. Fathers are designed by God to excel in this regard. They are tasked by God with the responsibility of calling forth their children into their emerging destinies.

Mothers who are adept at building safe nests can have an especially difficult time adjusting to this shift of roles. A parent who is fear-based and accustomed to controlling every aspect of their child's life, finds this shift extremely challenging.

Also, *as a child reaches teen years, the parenting role shifts from teacher to coach.*

Teachers teach in a closed environment exerting control over every aspect of a student's behavior. On the other hand, coaches, through direct involvement, stand on the sidelines while the players play the game *for themselves*. The young players are learning essential skills in a supervised real-life environment.

This shift is again aptly illustrated by many bird species that break the psychological dependence of their young by bringing food near the nest but *not into* the nest. Through supervised trial and error, their young learn how to fly in order to reach their food. Soon they are ready to leave the nest for good.

The human species ought to train their teens in a similar manner.

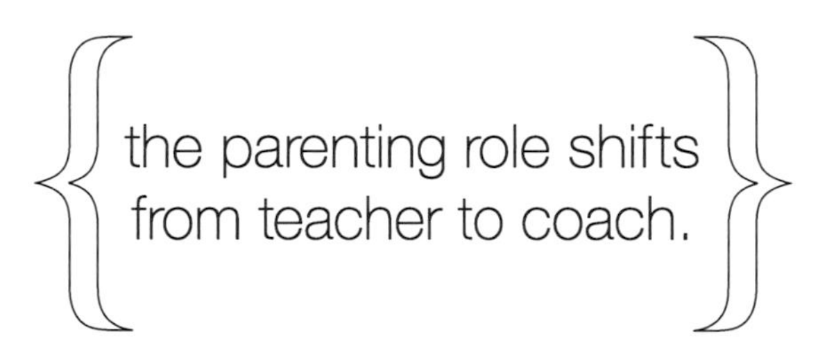

The teen years ought to be a transitional period when parents gradually teach their young how to look after themselves. Once they reach young adulthood, former teenagers ought to be ready to vacate the nest. In spite of financial security and sufficient education, that readiness to embark upon life's journey is often absent when the Family Blessing is missing.

When parents fail to notice

Sometimes, parents simply *fail to notice* the arrival of the new stage and therefore don't perceive the need to make any shift in the relationship with their children. The child, therefore, feels the shift before either parent realizes what is happening. In those moments, moms or dads can find themselves in conflict as they attempt to understand God's agenda for their child.

Apparently this even happened in Jesus' family!

When Jesus was almost 13 years of age, he and Mary exchanged words publicly revealing that Mary had yet to recognize the imminent transition taking place in her boy's life. The account of this conflict, in Luke 2:41-52, offers timeless insights for all parents of teens. The conversation between mother and Son is totally relevant to any parent who has had a conflict with an emerging teenager.

Jesus' family was once again on the way to Jerusalem for the biggest national celebration of the year – Passover. The event doubled as a family vacation for many. On the long, three-day walk from Nazareth, they would have been joined by friends and family who they perhaps might not have seen since the previous Passover. Year after year, those trips to Jerusalem would have been filled with familiar voices and traditional activities.

But this year Mary and Joseph failed to notice an important difference; Jesus was no longer a young child. A subtle shift was taking place in His body, and also in His mind. Pre-occupied with the need to prepare for His destiny, Jesus stayed behind to join the temple court debates.

Experimentation mistaken for rebellion

When Mary and Joseph left the festival, they assumed Jesus was in the company of relatives and didn't miss Him for a day. Not until three days later did they discover Him sitting in the middle of a circle of rabbis answering questions with such insight that everyone listening was amazed – *everyone except Mary and Joseph*. They were not interested in His scriptural knowledge at that moment. Jesus had appeared to act uncharacteristically, without parental consent, and they were more than a little perturbed.

Like any mother, Mary had feared for her Son's safety. Now that she and Joseph had found Him, that fear gave way to anger.

> teens often receive more recognition for their gifts and talents outside their family circle than from within.

We don't know whether Jesus had made an attempt to get the word to His mother that He was staying behind, however we *do know* that He had to do what He was doing. He was preparing for His destiny. Unfortunately the *urgent* took precedence over the *important* when Joseph and Mary found Jesus.

Mary interrupted the Bible class abruptly: "*Son why have you treated us like this*?"

Without waiting until they were alone, Mary scolded Jesus in public. Because Mary and Joseph failed to recognize that their Son was engaged in important preparation for His life's calling, He received public criticism instead of public affirmation. It would have been much better for Mary to affirm His gift in public and deal with the misunderstanding in private.

Jesus' interaction with His parents demonstrates a common occurrence – that teens often receive more recognition for their gifts and talents outside their family circle than within. The answer to the question, Do I have what it takes, requires affirmation that is too often absent in a teen's own home.

Unlike most teens, Jesus immediately addressed the core of the misunderstanding. When Mary said, "Your father and I..." Jesus turned His attention from the rabbis and reminded Mary who His *real* Father is.

Unlike many parents, Mary listened to her Son, and, "treasured all these things in her heart"*(Luke 2:51).*

The conclusion to this parent/teen episode comes as no surprise: Jesus submitted to His parents even though they didn't give Him what He required for the moment. As a result, mom, step-dad and Son launched out together on the long walk home with plenty of time to straighten it all out.

In a family of today, things could have turned ugly. Teenagers long for adults to listen to them without judging them. It is a form of honor. However when a child is dishonored and responds with rebellion, the devil's trap is sprung in their lives to grip their emotions and effectively block the blessing.

Often that is the moment when life-long addictions or destructive habits take root. Anger weakens self control, and young people often choose harmful substitutes for the sense of well-being that they are missing. Their identities become cursed and their destinies clouded until the lies are removed from their hearts.

Let's turn to some up-to-date examples of why this happens and how receiving a missed blessing can turn things around for good.

Neglect: Jane tells a story of the consequences of neglect at a fragile time in her life. The Lord Himself imparted the missed blessing to her during ministry time in one of our Blessings Workshops:

> *I was the youngest of five children in a very authoritarian home. I always wondered why I had fond memories of my father up to grade six, and why after that everything in my life seemed to go wrong for about the next eight years (including a teen pregnancy).*
>
> *When we were praying about my lack of blessing at puberty, immediately I remembered a time when I was really proud to be one of the only girls in seventh grade to qualify for the school gymnastics team. Most team members were two or three years older. We had a special assembly one evening so our parents could attend. I remembered being on the trampoline warming up and looking into the stands to see an empty seat beside my mother. Dad couldn't make the time to come see me. He just sat at home in his rocking chair that evening. That hurt.*
>
> *I felt unworthy and not valued. As we prayed, I realized that it was immediately after that disappointment that I dropped out of swim team, cross country and just about every other sport I truly loved. That was the moment rebellion entered my life, and now I understand why I always felt I became a totally different person in seventh grade.*
>
> *As I prayed with my eyes closed remembering this scene, I asked the Lord to show me where He was in all of this. In my mind's eye I was startled to see Jesus standing at the foot of the trampoline in a white robe with His hands up spotting me and a huge smile on His face. I was overwhelmed with a*

> *feeling of love and value. The Lord is so awesome. To top it off, this breakthrough came on the same day that I had volunteered to coach a girls' volleyball team for 7th and 8th graders! I am so amazed at His faithfulness.*

Jane's life took a sudden turn for the worse when she was dishonored through neglect. Jane's father had abdicated his role at the most critical time in his daughter's life. At the very moment she required affirmation, the devil's trap was sprung in her life because she returned rebellion for dishonor.

Jane suffered the consequences of her own rebellion for a number of years and cursed her own self worth as she willingly participated in destructive behavior. Although her lifestyle had now changed, Jane was still carrying an empty space in her heart reserved for a father's blessing, until the Lord himself showed up to fill that void.

Every *breakthrough* requires a *follow-through*. After gathering around Jane to affirm her new spiritual insights, we encouraged some of her close friends to seal this blessing by continuing to walk with Jane and to speak encouragement into her life.

Criticism: Jane's tragic struggle was the product of mere neglect. However many children have to battle a more deliberate foe to their identity which is *constant criticism.*

Ironically, criticism is usually given in the name of encouragement.

Parents mistakenly think that their words of correction are encouraging better performance.

We are reminded of the father who responded to his daughter's 97 percent average in school with the question, "Where are the other three marks?"

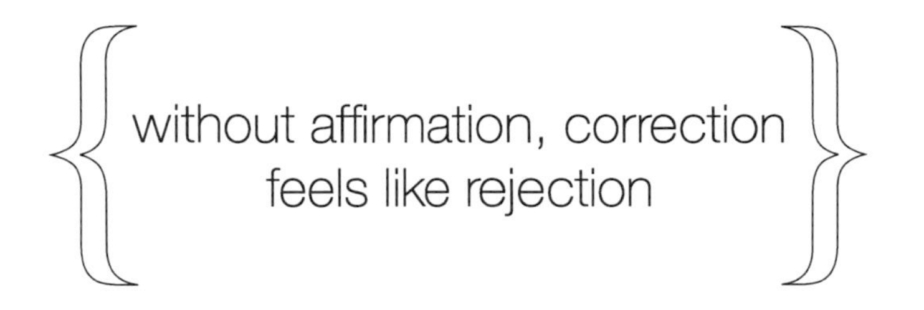

He presumed that 100 percent would bring exceptional opportunities for scholarships. However what the father meant, and what the daughter heard, were virtual opposites. She received the message that even her best efforts weren't good enough. When her dad criticized her marks, *he also crushed her motivation.* His words opened her heart to an act of rebellion that detoured her journey away from her God-given destiny for many years.

Remember, that without affirmation, correction feels like rejection. Correction without affirmation will hinder your teen's ability to answer the critical life-question, Do I have what it takes to make it?

What about single moms?

One of the curious things to note in the passage we were discussing earlier (see Luke 2) comes from the following observation – though he was present, *there is no record of Joseph entering into the conversation.* We don't know what he was doing while Mary was publicly confronting their boy, but it appears as if Mary did the talking for the two of them. Mothers too often have to take the initiative to discipline or interact with their teens without adequate assistance from their mate.

Right about now we can hear some single moms sighing in despair as they consider the monumental task of trying to walk with sons and daughters through teen years without a father in sight. God didn't intend for you to do this without the help of a male mentor in your children's lives. We counsel you to do whatever it takes to bring your children under positive godly influences from male role models during these critical years. To assist you, we have devoted an entire chapter to single moms in the third section of this book.

The value of ceremony at this stage

The Jewish culture has always understood the importance of ceremony to mark every important transition in life. The ancient rite of passage called *bar mitzvah* (for boys) and *bat mitzvah* (for girls) is a key element in the maturation of every orthodox Jewish child.

> Even simple ceremonies and traditions can effectively seal a blessing

Today some non-Jewish parents have begun to emulate this tradition with a ceremony that is often referred to as a Bar/Bat Barakah (son/daughter of blessing). We have included detailed explanations and inspiring examples of these in the next chapter entitled "Rites of Passage at Teen Years."

Even simple ceremonies and traditions can effectively seal a blessing of value and worth. A valued tradition in our home was the father-daughter "date" that spanned Jessica's entire school age years. These were special, and often formal, occasions that Terry used to model how a man should treat a woman. He would finish each date with the words, "*Don't give your heart away until you meet a man who treats you this well.*"

Birthday parties at any age can be used to impart blessing. We threw a surprise blessing party for our eldest son when he was 16 years of age.

When blessing doesn't seem to work

Regardless of how diligently parents communicate worth and value to their children, or how well they communicate blessing, it is still possible for children to rebel.

A teenager whom we know well was in her mid-teens when she

went through a time of rebellion against God and the values she had been taught as a child.

During this time her mother felt forewarned by the Holy Spirit to "hold the line" and not overreact. Mom and dad were not aware of everything their daughter was doing, however it was obvious that she had temporarily lost interest in her faith. Although they did not condone the rebellious behavior, they kept loving and blessing their daughter, and waited it out. With God-given authority over her life, her parents prayed in agreement that the pleasure of sin would soon be abated. In a fairly brief time, it was.

When she eventually disclosed her secret lifestyle, her parents' unconditional love helped melt her rebellious heart, and her life began to turn around. In fact, she wrote the following note to her parents to explain why even a blessed child can wander from the truth at times:

> *Teenagers have a weak point. It is fear. The devil pours into young girls and guys a fear of consequences, disapproval, and disappointment, especially in the teen years.*
>
> *I was entombed in fear that whatever I had done would cause me ruin if I confessed. I always had my parents blessing, but fear kept me from understanding the great love that is a product of parental blessing.*
>
> *I became a slave to my own deceit. Satan had me convinced that the last two people I could ever run to for safety on this earth were my parents. In fact, nothing was farther from the truth.*
>
> *When I finally told my parents all that had happened, I felt more loved than ever before. The elation, when we run back into the arms of God and those whom he has put as guardians over us, abounds to cover all sin. There is freedom in receiving and giving God's blessing. It is beneficial to let your kids know that no matter what they've done, they will be received in your love and forgiveness.*

We know this story is true in every detail because this teen's name is Jessica, and we are her parents.

Her life has never been the same since. After turning her heart back to Jesus, she led many of her friends to Christ. Two years later we had a blessing party for a dozen of them in our home.

Your story may be different from ours. You may have to endure longer than we did. But we can assure you, that the blessing you give your child during these years will eventually prevail.

ENDNOTE 1 Jim Valvano was a recruiter, motivator, and the beloved coach of the North Carolina State basketball team. He died in 1993 at 47 years of age.

CHAPTER 11

Adulthood

What am I called to do in this world?
Who will share my journey?

"Jesus was baptized too. And as He was praying, heaven was opened ...and a voice came from heaven 'You are my beloved Son and I am fully pleased with you' "

Luke 3:22 NLT.

"Heaven was opened"!

What a beautiful word picture of living in God's favor where God's presence is frequently felt and answers to prayer are frequently seen:

› a world where there is open communication with a heavenly Father who is committed to our wellbeing;

› a world where God's supply meets our every need (see Philippians 4:19).

Is it possible to live in such a world? We believe it is, and we believe that the blessing God intends for you to receive at adulthood helps to open the storehouse of heaven where your spiritual blessings are waiting (see Ephesians 1:3) to be released upon you here on earth. The heavenly Father isn't holding back every good and perfect gift until we get to heaven. We like to say it this way: *A Christian's life should not just be "pie in the sky when you die," but "steak on the plate while you wait!"*

When you walk in your God-given destiny, you can expect God to open the heavens above you and give you the resources you need to carry out your task. We've seen it happen time and time again. Unfortunately too many people reach adulthood without the kind of family blessing that enables them to understand who they really are in God's eyes and what they are truly capable of accomplishing.

Len, a 30-year-old, came to our church for counseling. He looked the part of a successful man, yet he simply could not keep a job or a girlfriend for any length of time. The reason for his restlessness became quickly evident as he shared his story.

Len had just completed a house that he had built virtually by himself. The framing, the electrical, the plumbing – he did it all, but not just to save money. Something other than money was motivating him.

When the house was completed, Len brought his father to the house site and gave him the grand tour explaining every detail of what he had done and how he had done it. His dad said nothing until the end of the tour. Proudly, Len turned to his dad, "Well dad, what do you think?" His dad paused and then listed everything in the construction that his son could have done better. No praise, no affirmation.

Len buried his head in his hands and moaned, "I built that house all by myself just to prove to my dad that I could do it. Why won't he ever tell me I have done a good job?"

For Len, the heavens seemed as brass. Anxious and overdue to begin his adult journey, he longed to hear, That's my boy! from the man who mattered most in his life. Until Len received the affirmation he desired through a father's blessing, his destiny was "on hold."

Family Blessing isn't a reward. It's a gift. When parents use that blessing as a reward for good behavior, they miss the point in a terrible way. When parents *withhold blessing* as a means of correction or motivation for their children, as did Len's dad, it produces the opposite effect from what they expect.

When the heavens open

Contrast Len's experience with that of another 30-year-old named Jesus (see Luke chapter 3).

At the time, Jesus' cousin John was at the forefront of a national spiritual revival as he led untold numbers through a baptism of repentance. The spiritual atmosphere was charged with expectancy that Israel's Messiah would soon be revealed. The magnitude of the revival was reflected by the fact that even unlikely candidates, such as tax collectors and soldiers, made the long trek to the Jordan river to be a part of what God was doing through John.

> Jesus received affirmation from His Father before He began His ministry...

Jesus also made the trek and insisted on going through the same baptism as everyone else. No one in the crowd knew Jesus' true identity yet, but God used Jesus' baptism as the ceremonial backdrop for a heavenly impartation. Jesus' Father had prepared a special time and a special place where to give His Son a blessing.

As John baptized Jesus, the heavens opened above Him and two things happened (see Luke 3:21-22):

- His Father extended "a meaningful touch" to Him through the manifestation of the Holy Spirit in the bodily form of a dove that landed upon Jesus;
- His Father spoke a message in an audible voice that "attached a high value" to Jesus saying, "You are my beloved Son in whom I am fully pleased."

Regardless of whether anyone else heard the heavenly voice that day, the words were meant for one person – they flowed directly from the Father's heart to His Son. The words, "You are" and "I am fully pleased," represented an unqualified affirmation upon Jesus' character. In essence, the Father was saying to His Son, "I have watched your character growth and I am happy with it. I am proud of who you have become."

Jesus received this affirmation of His character as a gift from His Father before He began His ministry! He had not yet performed one miracle; He hadn't preached one sermon, and hadn't picked one disciple. Yet He was already walking in God's favor under an open heaven. His Father's confidence in Him gave Jesus complete confidence that He was ready to fulfill the purpose for which He had come to earth. As we watch Jesus' life through the gospel accounts, it becomes evident that He never lacked God's supply even for a minute.

While the blessing of the Lord is bound to bring a measure of financial wellbeing in addition to spiritual benefits (see Proverbs 10:22), it does not always follow that blessing immediately brings material wealth. Prayers of blessing don't somehow exempt us from hard work, nor do they hold the promise for financial wealth that exceeds our talents. However a happy and secure adult who knows they are blessed has a far better chance of making good choices and succeeding in everything to which they apply themselves.

When ceremonies become celebrations

Jesus received another aspect of the blessing at His baptism. His Father not only affirmed His character publicly, but John publicly announced His coming ministry. John proclaimed Jesus' calling to the crowd saying, "Look – the lamb of God who takes away the sin of the world" *(John 1:29)*. This was a big event. Huge crowds of spiritually hungry people had come to listen to John who they knew was preparing the way for the Messiah. Jesus could have received no higher commendation and no one was more qualified to give it than John.

Having announced Jesus' ministry, John stepped aside and gave Him pre-eminence (see John 3:30). Jesus received the honor due His unique identity and destiny. What a celebration they must have had that day!

Today, graduation ceremonies and wedding ceremonies represent excellent opportunities for imparting blessing to young adults because they mark significant transition points in life. A graduation embraces a life calling, and a wedding, a life companion. Both should be turned into celebrations that seal the blessing released into the young adults' lives.

It works well for many family members and friends to speak into the lives of the bride and groom, especially for a first time marriage of two young people. Wedding receptions are ideal for speaking meaningful words that can be delivered in the form of a public blessing.

In our years of pastoring we have attended far too many receptions where a father or mother failed to use the opportunity wisely. We are incredulous to see embarrassed parents offer a few seconds worth of trite comments followed by awkward speeches full of attempted humor. Parents ought never to miss this opportunity to affirm a young person's life and to speak blessing over their future.

We have also noticed that hidden hurts can remain in a person's life for years when family members or close friends fail to attend a wedding. *Never underestimate the value of your presence at key celebrations in the lives of people you know.*

When the young leave the nest

When Jesus left the site of His baptism, He didn't return to live at home with His parents in Nazareth. He was led by the Spirit to go a different direction.

It is scripturally correct for young adults to leave their family home and launch out on a life of their own. For example, the Bible makes it clear that when a man marries, he will "leave his mother and father" and become one flesh with his wife (see Ephesians 5:31). The old English word used in the *American Standard Version* of the Bible is *cleave* which means *cling to.*

We have witnessed couples in their middle-aged years still hindered from union with their spouse because they are bound with emotional ties to controlling parents.

Our experience allows us to say that you cannot overestimate the value of ensuring that young adults are properly blessed as they leave their parents' home to establish a career and home of their own.

Parents need to communicate the following through blessing to a child who is leaving home for college or to be married:

› God is with you – an opening of heaven over their lives to enable them to prosper fully;

› You're going to make it – an affirmation of the child's readiness to take on the world;

› We're always here for you when you need us – an assurance that the parent will be available for consultation.

Without this blessing most young adults spend their 20s in what we call "trial and error" mode – trying this and that while they learn to discover who they are and what they may be good at. When a young adult leaves home with these truths deeply embedded in their soul, their life dreams will not be constantly threatened by insecurity. They will not be detoured from their destiny while attempting to prove their worth or competence. They will be excited and eager to get on with the adventure that they know God has called them to live.

Parenting roles shift - *again*

During adolescence parenting roles shift from teacher to coach.

When adult children leave their family home, parenting roles shift again – this time from coach to consultant.

There is a difference between a *coach* and a *consultant*. Unlike a coach who has the right to give advice and instruction to his players whenever he chooses, a consultant gives advice when only when *consulted*. No unsolicited advice and correction takes place! But too many parents won't let their children go, and cripple their child's ability to embrace the future.

A remarkably successful and bright young woman who was beginning to thrive in her career met with road blocks from a controlling parent. Her happy demeanor hid the turmoil inside. On one of the days that she was attending a Blessings Workshop, Melissa felt to pray on behalf of young adults whose parents needed to "untie the apron strings." We were unaware of any visible results, but when we returned home that evening an email awaited.

> *God used your session today in a powerful way. It is a watershed moment in my life. I feel God is releasing me into my calling and destiny to stand for truth and righteousness in my chosen field of work.*
> *My father was absent during important times of my life and my mother is rather controlling and has never fully released me as an adult because of her fears and overprotective nature.*
>
> *Melissa's prayer at the end concerning controlling mothers who didn't see what God is doing in different stages of life, related to me directly. So did Terry's prayers concerning absent fathers.*
>
> *I have renewed faith to believe that God is going to do something different and powerful in my life in the coming days. It's so timely, since my boyfriend and I are praying about marriage and even the possibility of working overseas.*

The prayer of blessing brought heaven's perspective to this young life and gave her the ability to apprehend her own future with confidence.

When marriage partners need blessing
It is more than just a point of interest to note that some of Jesus' greatest opposition came from the people who were the most closely related to him. Likewise some of the greatest challenges we face come from within our own home. Unfortunately, those who enter marriage without sufficient blessing in their lives often revert to patterns of dishonor once the honeymoon is over. The result will be a "bent" relationship pattern with their spouse:

- either they will "bend" *toward* the other person and present them with their unpaid emotional bills from past hurts;
- or they will "bend" *away* from the other person avoiding intimacy in a vain attempt to prevent further emotional pain.

Some couples live in pretence, looking and behaving like a normal couple while at least one or both are living a life of quiet desperation.

We call this state of relationship, "married singles."
In praying with couples, we have come to realize that marriage problems are often the result of each partner's lack of blessing manifest in a close relationship. When we are able to assist each partner to identify and recover their missed blessings, then their marriage immediately begins to improve.

The real challenge has been in helping people *desire* change at any cost, and there *is* a cost.

Part of that cost is a *willingness to forgive.* Whatever your family situation, your healing entails learning to give and receive forgiveness and to replace embedded lies with the truth. Whether it be a parent, spouse, or a former spouse, we must forgive them even of they do not give us what we feel we deserve or need. Without forgiveness heaven closes and blessing is blocked.

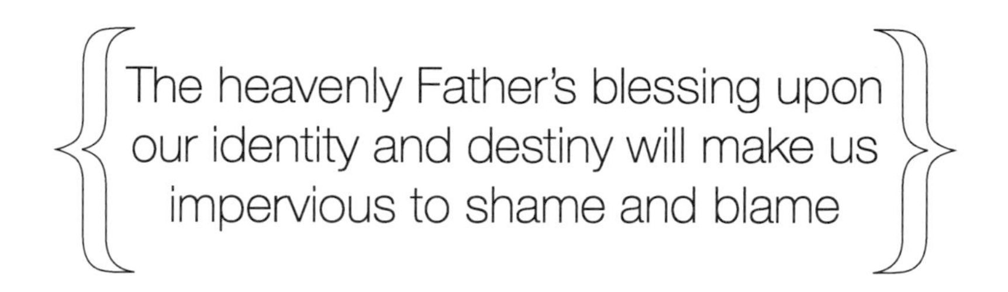

When trials come
Living under an open heaven is not to be confused with living a problem-free life.

Jesus often experienced opposition and misunderstanding. Immediately after His Father blessed His identity, Jesus retreated to the wilderness and experienced an attack on His identity from Satan himself. As soon as He returned from the wilderness to His home town of Nazareth, He experienced total rejection, to the extent that some people He had known all His life attempted to kill Him.

Likewise, when we are subject to spiritual attack through temptation or personal rejection by people who ought to treat us better, it is essential that we know deep down inside who we are in God's eyes. The heavenly Father's blessing upon our identity and destiny will make us impervious to shame and blame. When that truth is embedded within our hearts, we will be able to keep a proper perspective and resist the lies that come against us.

When dad can't speak the blessing
The truth is that many of us will never hear, That's my boy! or, That's my girl! from our earthly fathers and mothers.

This begs the question, If our parents cannot, or did not, bless us in marriage, can we be a good marriage partner?

The answer is "yes", however it's *conditional upon our humble willingness to acknowledge our need and seek the missed blessings.* The heavenly Father is more than willing to use other ways and means to bless us when parents are no longer able or willing.

Terry has a story to tell about this:

> *Before I discovered the principles of biblical blessing, I was preaching on the subject of emotional wholeness. When I finished my sermon, a counselor-friend came to me and said, "I can tell that you never received your father's blessing." I was stunned. How did he know?*
>
> *Something in my message had tipped off this astute man about the unfinished business in my heart. One simple statement had uncovered an unfulfilled longing – an emotional "loose end" that still required the touch of God.*
>
> *Although my father was a loving and kind man, he never demonstrated a personal relationship with Jesus Christ. He also died suddenly from a heart attack just one month after I was called into full time ministry. If he hadn't died, I doubt He would have blessed my career move.*
>
> *Ironically, my father had lived for more than 50 years without discovering the purpose for God had placed me, his son, on this earth. This unresolved emotional issue remained buried in my heart. It was an invisible yet influential factor in my emotional responses.*
>
> *Because the counselor and I were friends, I was willing to give him permission to speak into my life. He knew from his own experience what I was dealing with and he did for me what someone else had done for him. In a simple ceremony that included meaningful touch in the form of a gigantic bear hug, he called me forth as a man of God, speaking words of affirmation based upon his knowledge of my life and enhanced by direct insights given him by the Holy Spirit.*
>
> *It settled something deep within. It was more than a heartfelt wish from a friend – it was a spiritual truth deposited in my soul.*
>
> *That one event was a key turning point, but it didn't finish*

the task. Since that time I have heard words of affirmation spoken directly to my heart by God's Holy Spirit and by others at key moments in my life.

Recovering the missed father's blessing in Terry's life has certainly improved our marriage and helped us to be much more understanding of those who struggle in this area.

Be encouraged, and receive the truth that God is not limited by your family faults. He can take you from where you are, to wherever He wants you to go. Ask for the grace and the courage to recognize and receive the blessings you have missed and watch what it does immediately to improve your marriage and family relationships.

When someone you know needs an open heaven

We find great joy in helping others find the blessings they have missed, especially young adults who are reaching out for spiritual mothers and fathers in their walk with God.

Kristy, for example, is a vivacious young woman who discovered that the world was not giving her the answers she needed in life. Her drive for love and acceptance had led her on a fruitless search in many directions until she became hungry for spiritual reality. Our daughter's friend led her to faith in Jesus Christ. We realized that Kristy had not yet understood or received blessing on her new identity as a young Christian adult. She eagerly accepted our offer to give her the missed Family Blessing.

We knew Kristy well enough to speak words of personal affirmation upon her character and to picture a special future for her life. We also told her the meaning of her name and spent time praying with her. A couple of days later we received a card from her with these words:

> *Thank you for such an amazing experience.... I cannot tell you how much it meant. You have both encouraged me to find out who I really am, and...without those words of wisdom I would not be as overjoyed and content as I am today. Thank you again so much for a special day I will never forget.*

Something supernatural occurred in Kristy's soul. As we spoke words from our heart, the dove of the Holy Spirit descended upon her heart with a magnificent and gentle touch.

You can do this too for someone you love. If you provide the words, The heavenly Father will provide the "dove" of His presence.

CHAPTER 12

Senior Years

Am I Still Needed in this World?

"Her husband is respected at the city gate, where he takes his seat among the elders of the land Her children rise up and call her blessed"

Proverbs 31:23.

"The glory of young men is their strength, gray hair the splendor of the old"

Proverbs 20:29 NIV.

At the "ripe-old-age" of 50, friends of ours sold their business and moved to Africa to work as volunteer missionaries. The husband was prematurely gray. In fact he sported a head of completely white hair, which brought instant respect among the people group they served! Not so in North America where we live. The North American culture idolizes youthfulness and fears old age. Age and wisdom take a backseat to youth and physical beauty.

A truly blessed life as a senior adult needs purpose as much as pleasure

Commercials promote a "Freedom 55" lifestyle of playing golf, cruising the Caribbean, or roaming the continent in an RV. Yet even if this carefree lifestyle is attainable, a major life question still arises from deep within the heart: Am I still needed in this world?

A truly blessed life as a senior adult needs purpose as much as pleasure, and that purpose is found in playing a meaningful role in the lives of the younger generations.

Sitting in the gate

In biblical times people often lived in walled towns or cities. Many worked in the fields outside the walls all day and then came inside at night for protection. When people reached their senior years they were no longer expected to contribute to the city through hard work, and thus ceased their labor in the fields. Now they were valued for a lifetime of accumulated wisdom.

Some seniors were given a seat of honor at the city gate providing them with a "courtside" view of all the action. The purpose was more than just socializing. The elders of the city gathered there to oversee business transactions and settle disputes. Gatekeepers relied on the watchful eye of the elders to notice the comings and goings of all who passed through the gates, especially strangers.

Those who weren't given an official position in the gate of the city were still given the same kind of honor within their own families. Their life purpose was to pour the remainder of their lives into helping the next generation succeed.

Jesus did not live long enough on earth to become a senior, however after completing His life's work on earth, He returned to be seated at the right hand of God. He now rests from His labors, and is highly honored for His sacrificial life. He occupies the highest seat of authority from which He keeps watch over the world and constantly prays for the saints who are His true followers (see Hebrews 7:25-8:1).

In basketball terms, those who demonstrate wisdom and faithfulness throughout their lives are like former players who ought to be given "courtside seats" for life. They may no longer be playing the game, but they can be kept close enough to continue to experience the thrill of what's happening on the court, and be able to offer their advice to the current players when asked.

Contrast this biblical pattern with the position of seniors in westernized cultures. We expect them to congregate together and leave the rest of us alone to get on with our busy lives. Churches often consign seniors to separate social functions where they can reminisce about the "good old days."

If older folk seem critical at times, perhaps it's because they once held vital roles, but now feel as if they have been discarded – very much like a former minister whom Terry met during a cross-country airline flight. Over the course of a few hours, the man revealed how much he disliked the large church he now attended. As a senior citizen, he felt he could not relate, so he chose to sit in the balcony each Sunday. He had become a *spectator* instead of a *participant*. His critical comments masked his feelings. No one wanted to hear what he had to say anymore. With no one seeking his advice or counsel, this man felt disconnected and useless in his home church.

What's wrong with this picture?

Perhaps this man's critical attitude was part of the problem. Nevertheless, it's tragic to see seniors sitting in the "balcony" instead of in the "gates." Ignoring such a wealth of life experience is dishonoring to those who have paid with their lives to acquire it.

Seniors need ceremonies

Ceremonies can communicate a lifetime worth of honor and blessing. When appropriate honor is given to someone who has poured their life out for the good of others, then a blessing is imparted and closure is brought to that stage of their life. It is a misguided idea that "doing something for the Lord" means that you ought not be honored or thanked. Too often we have dishonored those who have labored among us by not publicly recognizing their sacrificial service. As a result they miss receiving a crucial life-blessing and it hurts, whether or not they are willing to admit it.

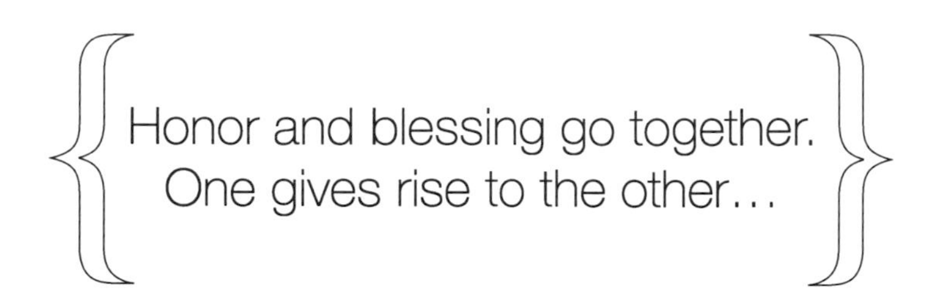

Terry was speaking at a leadership conference in South America. One of the other speakers was an American woman who, with her husband, had served as a missionary in a South American country for 39 years. During that time, she had acquired a nation-wide reputation for raising up indigenous full-time Christian workers. Recently she had retired, but had returned with her husband to South America to speak one more time to the Christian leaders whom she loved so deeply.

In a casual conversation, Terry asked what her mission board in America had done for her when she retired. "I received a paper certificate from the head office that said thanks for your 39 years of service," she replied.

Four decades of fruitful service with nation-wide impact, yet the sending agency failed to honor this couple with a ceremony, or any other public acknowledgment of their years of dedication! Apparently the office clerk who filled out the paper certificate hadn't even included the name of the country in which they had served. Unbelievable!

Coincidentally, Terry had planned to teach the leaders how to honor seniors. On the last day of the conference, unbeknownst to the missionary couple, he organized an informal ceremony to make up for the neglect of the mission board.

Having invited the couple to the podium, Terry addressed the 200 attendees and asked anyone among them who had been mentored by this couple to stand. About 20 pastors and leaders rose from their seats.

Terry then pronounced a blessing on the missionary couple, recounted their sacrifices, and praised them for the fruit of their labors represented by those standing. Each leader who was standing was invited to come forward and speak their own personal words of affirmation to the couple. The wife buried her head in her husband's shoulder and wept as decades of sacrificial love were finally honored appropriately. Everyone in attendance sensed a powerful presence of God. Evidently heaven was in agreement with the decision to publicly honor these humble servants.

"Her children rise up and call her blessed..."

Honor and blessing go together. One gives rise to the other. And nowhere do honor and blessing have a stronger connection than in the relationship between parents and children.

"Honor your mother and father," is the first of the ten commandments, and it ends with a promise: "You will live a long life, full of blessing" *(Ephesians 6:2-3 NLT).* The virtuous woman described in Proverbs 31 was honored by her children – "they arose and called her blessed."

These Scriptures tell us clearly that the initiative for blessing must shift from parents to children. It's up to the younger generation to initiate the words, deeds and ceremonies that will firmly establish honor and communicate worth and value in the lives of aging parents. The results can be wonderful.

One way to take initiative is through the celebration of anniversaries. At the 50th wedding anniversary of Melissa's parents, family from all over North America were invited. More than 40 came, including almost every member of the original wedding party. Special touches included skits, pictures and our daughter modeling her grandmother's wedding dress.

During the renewal-of-vows ceremony, we invited the honored couple to stand at the altar as they might have on their wedding day. This time, however, they were surrounded by their six adult children who in turn were encircled by 17 grandchildren. Terry led the children in a responsive reading that began with the words, "Today we rise up and call you blessed." The blessing included thanking the couple for choosing a lifestyle of giving first place to their family for half a century. It ended with the words, "As you are less able to take care of yourselves, we commit ourselves increasingly to look after your needs."

After we imparted this blessing to them, we saw some immediate fruit in the spiritual lives of some extended family members who were restored to a personal relationship with Jesus Christ.

Unexpected fruit can result from children blessing their parents. Ron and Christine were engrossed in careers, teenaged children, and needs of ailing parents at the time these events took place:

> *The homes we grew up in were quite similar. We were both accustomed to stern looks, criticism and very little praise. Meaningful touch, words blessing who we are, words calling us forth as a man or woman of God, words spoken into our identities and destinies – these elements of blessing were almost non-existent in our formative years. After attending a Blessings Workshop we resolved to bless our parents even though they didn't know how to express affirmation and blessing.*
>
> *Nevertheless, when our extended family gathered to celebrate significant milestones, we made a conscious effort to publicly express our gratitude to our parents and honor them for what they did right - a godly upbringing, support in our higher education, their hard work ethic, etc.*
>
> *Although we didn't see any change in our parents' attitudes toward us, we had planted seeds of blessing, and later we saw the harvest. A year later Ron's mother began to suffer with Alzheimer's disease and his father was diagnosed with lung cancer. This produced a "softening in his spirit." He began to relate to Ron in a way that he could not before.*
>
> *Ron was excited to finally be able to discuss his spiritual journey with his own father. This topic had always been "off limits." They wept and repented for pain they had caused*

each other. They discussed their mutual grief over a wife and a mother who is just not the same woman that she used to be. We have sown blessings into her life too and will continue to do so realizing that because of her disease we may never see the fruit – at least not on this side of heaven.

Then Ron's father called for his grandchildren to visit him for the last time. When they came he spoke privately to each about his love for them and how proud he was of them. He gave them a life blessing.

Christine was also struggling with unresolved issues in her relationship with Ron's dad. After 25 years, and with time running out, she was fearful that he still could not receive our love.

About four days before his death, the Spirit of God led Christine to ask for forgiveness, and to release blessing and honor over him. His response was, 'What did I do to deserve great kids like you?' Finally God had restored what had been stolen from our relationship. We felt released to arrange a very honoring funeral and sing as a family by his graveside, "Praise God from Whom All Blessings Flow."

At his funeral, Ron's father was honored by many people – from former refugees whom he had assisted, to elderly people with whom he had had opportunity to minister. We couldn't help but think how he had meant so much to so many people over the past number of years, yet he was more-or-less absent as a father and grandfather. However because of the acts of blessing that we performed, much reconciliation and healing occurred.

Now we had closure, and buried all resentments with his body. At the graveside with uncle, aunt and cousins we were able to model forgiveness, honor and blessing. We also used the occasion to bless our children by giving each one of them a family heirloom. God gets all the glory.

We are constantly amazed by God's timing. We have lost track of the number of times someone has heard this message and decided to make amends through blessing an important senior in their life – parent or otherwise – only to see that person pass on shortly afterwards. We can only conclude that the Family Blessing in senior years is somehow very important to God and His purposes in this life and perhaps in the life to come.

An old Salvation Army saying refers to people who die as having been "promoted to Glory." The blessing we can impart to those in their senior years will not only lay to rest longstanding relationship issues here on earth, but will also help to prepare them for eternal promotion!

PART THREE

Giving the Blessing

CHAPTER 13

Learning from the Pros

May the Lord protect and defend you.
May He always shield you from shame.
May you come to be
In Israel a shining name.

May God bless you and grant you long lives.
May the Lord fulfill our Sabbath prayer for you.
May God make you good mothers and wives.
May He send you husbands who will care for you.

May the Lord protect and defend you.
May the Lord preserve you from pain.
Favor them, Oh Lord, with happiness and peace.
Oh, hear our Sabbath prayer. Amen.

From the Sabbath Blessing by Tevye and Golde
for their daughters in *Fiddler on the Roof.*[1]

When we teach a Family Blessing seminar, we often ask if anyone in the audience grew up in a family in which they received a spoken blessing on a regular basis. It's rare to see a hand raised in response. Those who claim to have *ever* received such a blessing from their parents in their entire childhood are in the minority. Yet in an observant Jewish family, most children receive a personal blessing nearly a thousand times before they leave their parents' home. It's not hard to conclude that Jewish families are in a league of their own when it comes to this topic. You could say they are "pros" on the subject.

Blessing is in the "DNA" of a Jewish family. Their physical existence is a direct result of God's promise to bless Abraham. Jewish identity is deeply rooted in the biblical account of the way in which Abraham's blessing was passed along from generation to generation in spite of many obstacles. Since that time, a faithful remnant of Jews has continued to pass this Family Blessing on to succeeding generations for more than 3,000 years.

The Sabbath blessing

One of the most well known expressions of the Jewish Family Blessing is the Shabbat (Sabbath) blessing which typically occurs after sundown each Friday night. It is spoken to children as part of a weekly ceremony that follows ancient tradition, but also leaves room for individual expression.

Here is an excerpt from a modern day guide:

> *There are many variations on how the blessing is made. The most common custom is for the father to put his hands on the child's head and recite the blessing. (In some homes the mother gives the blessing with the father, or even instead of the father). In some homes the blessing is followed by a kiss, and in other homes it is followed by personal words of praise. In some homes each child gets up at the table and stands before the parent to get the blessing, and in other homes the parent walks around the table and blesses each seated child, often praising some accomplishment in his or her week.*

Whatever procedure is followed, the blessing is sure to make the child feel special and loved, boost the child's self-esteem, and give the child fond memories of Shabbat family together time.[2]

One reason for the effectiveness of the Shabbat blessing over the centuries is that *it is not a stand-alone event.* It is ensconced in the Sabbath tradition which ensures that families observe it without fail on a weekly basis.

Parents who are serious about creating a blessing legacy can learn much from this tradition

Another reason for its effectiveness is found in the manner in which the Sabbath is observed. It is a day filled with meaningful symbols, songs, foods and prayers – a marvelous blend of words, deeds and ceremonies woven into a three-fold cord that, despite all attempts, could not be broken (for examples visit the website www.aish.com).

Parents who are serious about creating a blessing legacy can learn much from this tradition. Regular family times set aside for celebration and blessing are a fundamental component. But because we live in a frenetic culture that has little or no appreciation for the value of Sabbath rest, creative methods may be required for gathering family members together on a regular basis. Those who persevere reap tremendous rewards.

A third reason for the success of the Shabbat blessing relates to the personal connection the Jews have with biblical figures from the past. Out of curiosity one day I casually asked a Jewish friend, "Yaffa, where do you come from?" I expected her to respond with the city or region of her birth. Instead she turned to me with a puzzled look and exclaimed, "You have read the Bible and you don't know the answer? Why, I come from Abraham, *of course!*"

Yaffa's response highlights a significant truth. The Jewish people have a connection with their roots that is completely foreign to most Gentiles (the biblical term for non-Jews). Jewish people read the Old Testament like a family journal, and indeed it is. We Gentiles can easily overlook the rich family application in these stories because we don't identify with the biblical figures as our personal ancestors. However, through faith in Christ we can all lay claim to the *spiritual* blessings given to Abraham's descendants (see Romans 4:16). Any parent can invoke the qualities of biblical characters for their children through a spoken blessing! We intentionally named our first child David after the biblical hero King David. We have often used the King's character qualities when forming a blessing for our son.

Connecting with your own heritage

While it is true that biblical heroes provide a rich source of character qualities from which we can draw, we also highly recommend that you search *your own* family heritage. Ancestral information is often no more than a curiosity for many of us. As a result we fail to discover potential blessings that remain hidden like a can of preserves in the family cellar. When a person finally decides to investigate for themselves, it is surprising how often their research leads to the discovery of a "God story" in their family history. Here are two examples.

A minister named Bill attended a conference where we were the speakers. He experienced an ongoing struggle with his sense of identity which was rooted in the reminders he constantly received that he was an *illegitimate child* – a terrible term for children who were born outside of marriage.

During the conference Bill received personal ministry that helped him recover the early life-blessings he had missed. Following this, Bill researched his family history and, to his utter amazement, discovered in it several ministers of the gospel whose lives spanned several previous generations. This discovery helped erase and replace the lie in Bill's heart that he was an accident. Now he clearly saw the truth that he was chosen by God to perpetuate a family calling to full time Christian ministry.

Another example comes from a church leader named Penny who listened to our teaching on the subject of generational blessing. A few months later she wrote us an e-mail saying:

> *No one in my family knew the Lord, so it never dawned on me that I might have a godly heritage somewhere in my family line. One afternoon I asked my mom if we had any people of faith in our family history... She replied, "Yes." I had a cousin who was a pastor and second cousins who were missionaries... Even my grandmother had taught Sunday school before I was born.*
>
> *I did have a godly heritage in my own blood line! That knowledge in itself was a tremendous blessing to me.*

Like Penny and Bill, Terry also used to believe that he didn't have a spiritual heritage to celebrate. One day after he expressed that opinion in public, he felt a strong rebuke from the Holy Spirit. In Terry's mind he clearly heard the heard the words, "Stop that! You are dishonoring me." So we decided to research what we had assumed was a fairly barren spiritual history. To our surprise, we discovered hints of a rich heritage on the Bone side of the family line including ancestors who were named after John Wesley, the great English revival preacher and founder of Methodism.

About the same time that Terry's family history was coming to light, a chance meeting led us to discover that our church was near the site of an historical Methodist revival movement that took place during the time when Terry's ancestors lived in the same region. These facts combined with a prophetic word from a trusted source, revealed that contrary to Terry's life long belief about himself, he had a vibrant spiritual heritage. Terry explains how this impacted his life:

> *These moments of discovery uncovered a new aspect of my true identity and destiny. My new-found connection with my*

spiritual heritage profoundly impacted the way I think about myself. I sense a personal connection as I read the history of the Methodist movement. I also have a new level of confidence with which to bless my children.

Now when I lay my hands upon them, I invoke the generational blessing that is upon our family line.

Regardless of whether you discover any significant facts about your spiritual heritage from generations past, you yourself can begin a spiritual heritage that outlives you and lasts for generations to come. Do not minimize the value of simple family rituals that can be used as a platform for family blessing.

Let's get started

- Pray a prayer similar to the **Generational Blessing Prayer** found in Appendix A
- **Start your own traditions**: First take a few moments to think about any family rituals that have already been a valued part of your lives (e.g. family dinners or other shared activities). With a little forethought and planning any parent can turn certain aspects of the family routine into an opportunity to form a blessing tradition. You will need to examine your family schedule. What do you need to change so you have time to give blessings to your children regularly? What could you incorporate into a regular Family Blessing event? Which biblical characters could you use in crafting a blessing?

ENDNOTE 1 From the 1971 film adaptation of the 1964 Broadway musical of the same name. MGM studios. Directed by Norman Jewison.

ENDNOTE 2 Adapted from *Blessing the Children* by Lisa Katz ©2007 http://judaism.about.com/od/sabbathdayshabb2/qt/bless_children.htm. Used with permission from About, Inc. online at www.about.com. All rights reserved.

CHAPTER 14

How to Craft a Blessing

In Genesis 49 we read the account of how Jacob blessed his sons and grandsons who eventually became the patriarchs (fathers) of the 12 tribes of Israel.

You will notice that each blessing consisted of two parts. Jacob spoke to each child individually about his character and his future. Also, each blessing was carefully crafted for the specific child to whom he was speaking. Under the guidance of the Holy Spirit Jacob outlined their unique identity and destiny one by one.

> Even a poorly delivered blessing is much better than no blessing at all!

Similarly, to bless someone effectively you must have a measure of insight into their character and be able to perceive something about the positive future God intends for them. This insight comes through a combination of natural observation and spiritual revelation. When you deliver a spoken blessing, your goal is to recognize and verbalize the noteworthy characteristics of the recipient, and to articulate what you perceive God desires to do *in* their life and *through* their life in the future.

Perhaps you don't feel as self-confident as Jacob appears to have been when he eloquently blessed a dozen descendants on a single occasion. Often people who are not yet experienced at delivering a written or spoken blessing have a fear of making a mistake. That's understandable. But even a poorly delivered blessing is far better than no blessing at all!

The truth is that whenever you attempt to give someone a blessing, God agrees with your efforts. The Holy Spirit partners with your blessing to bring results that often go beyond your own words.

The five elements of a blessing

We have discovered a format that works well for any kind of blessing. It's from a book entitled *The Blessing* written by Gary Smalley and John Trent. In it, they outline five elements of a blessing:[1]

- a meaningful touch
- a spoken message
- attaching a high value
- picturing a special future
- an active commitment

Each of these elements is flexible according to the situation. Let's review each one briefly:

A meaningful touch may range from a handshake to a hug depending on the relationship between the participants and the occasion. Something powerful is communicated when a hand is laid upon the person being blessed. When we bless our children, I usually like for them to sit while I lay my hand on their head. The "laying on of hands" is also an important component during public blessing ceremonies.

A spoken message is the main substance upon which the blessing is built. A spoken blessing is more powerful when it is succinct. Write the text ahead of time so that you are confident that it reflects everything you wish to say concisely and clearly. It can be either in point form or verbatim. When it is time to pronounce these words, make direct eye contact with the person. You may first offer a few introductory words. Then, begin the blessing with phrases such as these (for additional examples of wording, see the appendices of this book):

- I bless the following characteristics in your life...
- May you be like (name a person), who was (name the characteristic)...
- I see God at work in your life in the following way...

If you cannot speak to the person directly, or face to face, your blessing can also be effective delivered in a written form.

Attaching a high value is a key component with which to begin a blessing. What do you see about the person's character that is worthy of praise? Your verbalization of the person's value, and the value you place upon your relationship with them, is a powerful tool for the Holy Spirit to use in counteracting lies and depositing truth deep into a person's heart.

Picturing a special future involves comprehending through observation and insight what God desires to do in and through the recipient's life. Insight comes through relationship *and* revelation. This point is especially important for parents to note. Only when parents have a clear understanding of the potential of their child, can they pronounce a blessing with confidence and authority. When preparing a blessing, be sure to ask God to give you insight regarding the person's future.

An active commitment refers to your commitment to your future relationship with the person. It is probably the most flexible aspect of the blessing. When a commitment is verbalized during a public blessing ceremony it becomes a promise. Words of commitment ought to be carefully planned beforehand and not spoken in the emotion of the moment. A promise of commitment made and broken can be damaging to the relationship and can weaken the effect of the spoken blessing. A safe way to express commitment is to indicate your availability to help and counsel whenever you are asked. Sometimes, however, an occasion warrants more than that. If you are not the one who will be following up with commitment toward the person after the blessing, then add a prayer asking God to provide the right person.

Using the five elements

A few years ago at a conference, after we taught on the subject of Family Blessing, one of the attendees was eager to speak to us. He wanted to bless his daughter on her wedding day and wasn't sure how to proceed. We gave him these five elements and encouraged him to use them as a skeletal structure to flesh out with his own creativity. A few weeks later we received the following response in an email:

> *My wife and I arrived back in town yesterday evening after our daughter's wedding. The father of the groom and I took about seven minutes in the ceremony to give the parental blessing. We followed the five elements outlined in* The Power of Blessing *book.*
>
> *We first spoke words of value about both the bride and groom. We then pronounced our blessing. We laid our hands on their shoulder for our meaningful touch. Then, speaking from a prepared text approximately one paragraph in length, we each told them how we would partner with them on their journey to blessing.*
>
> *Following that, we presented them with a study Bible which my son-in-law and I had picked out. I wanted it to be a Bible that would be used, so we chose* The Living Translation *in a study format. We had it imprinted, and while [we were] in the store a customer volunteered to write in the front in calligraphy.*
>
> *It was powerful – emotional! Everybody, including the 15 lawyers present (my son-in-law is a lawyer) and the officiating minister, commented on the uniqueness and the impact of the blessing. What you shared really provided the framework for what we did....*

We think that this story proves the power of blessing. After all, 15 lawyers can't be wrong at the same time! We rest our case!

Not every blessing requires a public ceremony, and mothers often play as much of a role as fathers in imparting blessing. In this instance we were impressed at how well the fathers had worked together to craft the details of this blessing. Whatever the occasion, We recommend that you build your blessing upon these five elements and adapt it to your unique situation.

The role of prayer

Remember that a blessing is not a prayer. Prayer ought to accompany a blessing, but it does not replace it. People who do not understand this will often revert to praying when asked to participate in a blessing ceremony. Typically, they bow their heads, close their eyes and ask God to bless the person for whom they are praying. However, asking God to bless someone is *not* the same as giving them a blessing yourself! A blessing should be spoken in the first person using direct eye contact. Prayer may then play a role as part of the active commitment that follows.

If you desire help to craft a blessing, you can review the samples and examples found in the appendices. Then print a copy of the Blessing Form found in Appendix A and follow these steps:

- Prayerfully choose a Scripture that conveys a positive message suitable to the person you wish to bless. Hint: look for ones that start with the phrase "May you..." or "May God..."
- Write a sentence or two describing something noteworthy that you have observed about this person's actions or character.
- Record words that describe this person's value in your eyes and in the sight of God.
- Add any good thing that you perceive God to be doing in their life right now.
- Describe the ways in which you believe this person can be used by God to encourage and bless others in the future.

› If appropriate, state how you are willing to assist this person to achieve the future you have pictured for them.

ENDNOTE 1 *page 27, The Blessing, 1986 Simon & Schuster New York, N.Y.*

CHAPTER 15

Rites of Passage at Teen Years

One of the most challenging transitions occurs at the "border crossing" from pre-teen to teen years. As a teenager's body attains sexual maturity, his or her mind begins to grasp for a new identity.

For centuries many cultures have addressed this transition by developing certain "rites of passage." In days gone by, a boy might have been required to perform great feats of skill in hunting or physical endurance to prove his manhood. Even today many cultures still employ ceremonies, most of which feature less exertion and more celebration. However, the purpose is the same – to mark the key transition from childhood to adulthood.

A *Bar Mitzvah*, which means "son of the commandment," or *Bat Mitzvah*, "daughter of the commandment," is completed by Jewish boys and girls between the ages of 12 and 14. When Jewish young people undergo their "*Bar/Bat Mitzvah,*" they assume the responsibilities of an adult under Jewish law: they are no longer innocent, and become responsible for their own actions (good or bad). The celebrations can be extremely elaborate.

The *Quinceañera* or *Quince Años* (meaning "15 years") is still practiced today in Latin America. This celebration marks the transition from childhood to womanhood. Traditions include giving and throwing a quince doll which signifies the young lady's last doll as a child. She throws it to the other female children in attendance, much as a bride throws a garter at a wedding reception. After the inaugural dance, the girl sits in a chair in the center of the dance floor, and her father removes her flats ("girls" shoes). He puts high heels on her feet, signifying her becoming a young lady (excerpted from http://en.wikipedia.org/wiki/Quinceanera).

The value of imparting a special blessing to young teens has largely been ignored in Western culture. It is heartening, therefore, to see many Christian families today rediscovering the value and effectiveness of individually-designed blessing events for their teens. This type of ceremony has become known to some as a *Bar/Bat Barakah* (son/daughter of blessing) ceremony, or a Christian *Bar/Bat Mitzvah.*

Three elements of a blessing ceremony

Whether these blessing events are simple or elaborate, they involve three basic elements:

1) *A period of instruction*: The event should be planned well in advance. Key to its success is the child's understanding and ability to embrace its purpose. Just as a teen being confirmed in a church is required to attend confirmation classes, so parents need to take time to cover topics important in the child's life and future with respect to blessing. Craig Hill, in his guidebook for parents, says that instruction should prepare the child for five things:[1]

- to enter into a settled sense of adult identity
- to enter into a clear sense of purpose and personal mission statement
- to be emotionally released into manhood or womanhood
- to take responsibility for his/her own spiritual health
- to walk in sexual purity all the days of his/her life

2) *The content of the ceremony*: A uniquely designed ceremony typically includes the following:

- an instructive word of encouragement from significant people in the child's life
- a verbal/written commitment from parents to the ongoing process of life coaching
- a response by the child reaffirming their commitment to

the Lord, along with a promise to honor their parents and to pursue their destiny

› an exchange of meaningful gifts such as a "promise ring" (from a father to his daughter) that represents her commitment to sexual purity.

3) ***The celebration*:** The ceremony is held in conjunction with a dinner, a party or other special event. It is advisable to include the child in planning so that the celebration reflects their desires.

Whatever form they may take, the common purpose of these ceremonies is to communicate value and worth, to affirm blessing on a child's gender, gifts and talents, and to call the child forth as an emerging adult.

It is naïve to imagine that a single ceremony, no matter how elaborate, can fulfill the function of transitioning a young person from child to adult. Teens must answer the life-question, Do I have what it takes to make it in this world? They will need continued encouragement throughout their adolescent years to adequately answer this question for themselves. A blessing ceremony is just the beginning.

Ideas for parents

Friends of ours, Rick and Cheryl, designed beautiful events for each of their two daughters. Here is how Rick describes the events and especially his role:

> *On their 13th birthdays I took each of our girls out for an evening in a way that fit their interests. I took one to the highest end restaurant in the city. I took the other for the best wings and ribs in town followed by a night at the theatre.*
>
> *Both of them received a ring, (as expensive as I could afford without being too excessive) to understand how valuable they are and how important their purity is to the heart of God. Once it was placed on their finger, it was not to come off until their wedding day (and so far it hasn't). I ensured that they*

fully knew before the night began what was coming, and were ready and wanting to make the commitment.

Then we also had individual blessing parties for each of them. It isn't a blessing if it doesn't connect with them, so I spent some time talking with my girls in advance introducing what we wanted to do and ascertaining what would make it spiritually significant for them. We found out who the people were in their lives that had made an impact on them from as early as they could remember to [the present], and invited as many as we could. I asked every person to prepare something to say that would bring the blessing of God to their lives.

Everything that was said was to be written out so that a scrapbook could be made for those days when the girls might question God's plan for their lives, as happens to all of us from time to time...(my one girl has a private drawer filled with words of encouragement and letters).

The meal was part of their plan as well...much like a birthday where they are the honored guest. One daughter wanted it all fancy and the other had a barbeque.... One dressy...one in blue jeans!

Jeff, another friend, planned a similar event for each of his two boys. He arranged with the school principal for his eldest son to be visited throughout the day by significant people in his life. He followed up this event with a special dinner during which a carefully selected group of ten men each spoke to the boy about a character trait of a godly man. Several of the guests also gave his son a meaningful gift or prayed for him.

Jeff planned a different kind of event for his other son. He took him on a walk through places significant to him from his own childhood and shared stories and lessons from his life. After this intimate time of fellowship, Jeff had arranged for a dinner party. People significant in his son's life were invited to attend the event.

No more secrets

Even though a parent carefully designs a meaningful blessing ceremony, they may encounter roadblocks that prevent teens from receiving the required blessing. As the old saying goes – honesty is the best policy. It is also an essential building block for blessing. Parents often believe that they are "protecting" their children by shielding them from family secrets. Sometimes the motivation is to cover shame. But as a child approaches teen years, withholding the truth becomes an act of dishonor.

As daunting as the task may seem in some situations, speaking the truth in love is a pre-requisite for successfully delivering a blessing. One family we know experienced this in a profound way:

Brenda and Sam approached Terry, after a workshop he was teaching, to share a family secret. Seventeen years prior, Brenda had conceived a child through an extra-marital affair. She had confessed to her husband, and he had agreed to keep the child and raise her as his own. Now, at 16 years of age, this daughter looked physically different from her siblings and had never felt she belonged in the family. She was starting to demonstrate rebellious behavior that no amount of parental effort could overcome.

Terry told them that they could not build a house of blessing on a foundation of lies. Until the daughter, Laura, was properly welcomed into their family based on her true identity, their attempts at blessing would be severely weakened. Terry recommended that they take her away for a weekend and during that time confess the truth.

Sam and Laura prayerfully followed through with this suggestion. They invited Laura to spend a weekend alone with them and allowed her to pick the location. She chose a mountainside retreat. Here's what happened in Brenda's words:

> *Our trip with Laura was one of the hardest things I have ever had to do. To sit there and tell my own daughter that I had had an affair and been unfaithful to her dad was not easy. Sam spoke to her first and told her what she meant to him. Then I read her a long letter listing all the things I love about her and how special God made her. I didn't realize how much*

> *love I had for her until that moment. We all cried and hugged and Laura listened very carefully. God gave us the words to say and the strength to tell her everything.*
>
> *Her first response was, "He's not my real Dad?" She appreciated our honesty and enjoyed the time alone with us. We both hugged and held her. She seemed relieved [because] she had known something was up, but now there was a peace in her spirit after we were finished talking.*
>
> *I knew for years that God had forgiven me, but until Laura was aware of the truth, I had no idea that freedom could feel so wonderful.*
>
> *Laura seems to be happier, and I am able to love her more than ever. She also is showing much more love for us. She made Sam a Father's Day card that brought tears to our eyes. She's going to be okay. God has set us free!*

Sam and Brenda did not stop there. They felt God wanted them to bring this situation completely into the light, so with Laura's permission they invited the rest of the children to a family meeting. They honored Laura and included her in the event planning. The date was set to coincide with Brenda and Sam's 25th wedding anniversary. Here is what happened, again in Brenda's words:

> *...that evening after supper, we told the children that we were going to have a family talk. They were all a bit nervous [because] they thought they were in trouble! I started off with verses from Ephesians which changed the mood. I told them that there was something their dad and I had kept from them, thinking it was the right thing. But now we realized that they needed to know.*
>
> *Sam explained to them what had happened and the role he played in it. He did an excellent job and I was so proud of him. The girls took it the hardest, and we made sure we let the kids know that Laura wanted them to know. We then asked them individually for forgiveness and each one of them*

lovingly responded with a yes. They were relieved at the fact that I didn't have to live with the lie anymore. They each went to Laura on their own afterwards and hugged her and said that she is their sister and nothing will ever change that. That was so good for Laura. I am so glad that there are no more secrets.

Terry wanted to know – did the blessing work? Had it produced lasting effects? He e-mailed Brenda more than a year later to find out, and here is how she replied:

... every time I reflect back to that time in my life, it shows me how great a God we have and how blessed our family really is; especially when everyday life isn't going so well. Laura is doing so much better. She has lots of friends and much joy...She is happy to be in our family.

In this day and age there are too many secrets that are damaging lives that could be so happy. For us it was the right thing to do to share it with Laura and our other children. God will continue to bless us because of this.

Sam and Brenda abandoned their shame and discovered that "where sin increased, grace increased all the more" *(Romans 5:20)*. May parents everywhere find the same courage to speak the truth in love so the blessing may be given.

Truth to go

Take time to pause and reflect. Are there any secrets in your family that may impede the giving and receiving of blessings? Do not allow shame or fear to keep you from bringing to light those situations that God's grace can turn into blessings.

Do you have children in their teen years who require a special blessing event? Prayerfully plan one using the examples in this chapter and the instructions in Appendix A.

A special note to parents who have performed a *Bar Barakah* ceremony with their teens: If your children have already experienced their Christian "rite of passage" blessing, then maybe it's time to send them on a mission trip or get them involved in some form of outreach event where they can strengthen their newfound sense of identity.

ENDNOTE 1 *Bar Barakah, A Parent's Guide to a Christian Bar Mitzvah,* Family Foundations International, Pg. 39.1998.)

CHAPTER 16

Blessing a Person's Name

"If the words we parents speak to our children have the power of life or death, then consider the phenomenal power resident in the one word we speak to them far more than any other – the word they will hear throughout their entire lives. I'm referring, of course, to a child's name"

Rolf Garborg.[1]

Nothing is more personal than a name.

It was the first gift your parents gave you. It will last your entire lifetime.

There is an inherent authority in the assigning of a name. God gave Adam authority to rule over the earth. Adam exercised that authority by fulfilling his God-given assignment of naming all the animals (see Genesis 2:20) Parents exercise the authority God gave Adam by naming their children. Naming is part of the stewardship of parenting, and because it is a great responsibility, parents should choose names for their children prayerfully and carefully. A name can bless, or sometimes curse, the identity of a child before they have an opportunity to discover who they are in God.

In biblical times, names were chosen to reflect identity as well as to prophesy destiny. A person was given a name that was connected to their nature, for example, "Abraham" means "father of a multitude."

One biblical story demonstrates the power of names to shape destiny. In a period of time when Israel was largely backslidden, one family boldly decided in faith to name their child Elijah, meaning "God is Great." Whenever his parents addressed him, Elijah heard the words "God is Great"! Imagine what that sounded like when to Elijah as a small child:

God is Great – eat your breakfast!
God is Great – put your clothes away!
God is Great – play nicely with your friends!

Could this be one of the reasons that Elijah's faith was so great when he faced the 450 prophets of Baal on Mount Carmel (see 1 Kings 18:20)? When he had to prove that the God of Israel was great, and immeasurably more powerful than Baal, perhaps he shrugged and thought to himself, No problem – God is Great!

These Bible stories are instructive for parents even today. In our family, we have always believed in the significance of names therefore we sought God's guidance when choosing the name for each of our three children. More than 25 years later, it is remarkable to observe how well our children's names fit their individual characters and life callings!

Discovering the meaning of a name

What happens when a child's name has been chosen without thought given to the relationship between the name and the child's identity? You may be surprised to discover how God can use a person's name to bestow His blessing. A remarkable example of this came from a friend of ours who forwarded the following e-mail after reading our teaching on the importance of names:

> *I hadn't thought of it before, but the story of our daughter's name has a spiritual meaning as a Name Blessing. My husband's name is Ken and I'm Daina. Before our daughter was born I was playing with combinations of our names to*

make a name for our daughter (I had made up my mind she would be a girl!). I came up with the name, Kenda (KEN and DAina). When she was born, we named her Kenda. Not long after, I was flipping through a baby name book when, to my surprise, I found the name Kenda. I learned that it is an American Indian name meaning, "child of the Living Waters"! Talk about God putting destiny in a name!

A Name Blessing does not always present itself so clearly or quickly as it did for Ken and Daina.

Research is often required to uncover a meaning that may have been previously unnoticed. Or sometimes the research will produce variations of meaning. In these situations, it is necessary to trust the leading of the Holy Spirit as you prayerfully choose the most relevant meaning.

Once in a while it may be difficult to find the meaning of a uniquely crafted, or unusual name. In this case we recommend finding a name that most closely resembles the sound of the person's actual name.

Another option when preparing to bless someone's name is to go beyond given names to research the surname (family name). Melissa discovered that the origin of her maiden name comes from a certain way of pronouncing *Luke.* This is significant to us as Melissa's main Bible teaching is derived from the gospel of Luke!

Redeeming the meaning of a Name

The Bible records that God frequently changed a person's name to identify that person more directly with their destiny. Abram (exalted father) became Abraham (father of a multitude). Simon became Peter, which means *rock.*

Jacob's name change could have factored in his desire to prevent his son Benjamin from carrying a name that would have been a curse. Of Jacob's 12 sons only two were born to Rachel – the wife he truly loved. The birth of Rachel's second son, Benjamin, was bittersweet because Rachel died in childbirth.

By this time his name was already changed from Jacob (deceiver) to Israel ("one who prevails with God"). Jacob fully understood the power of names to curse or bless. Moments before Rachel died giving birth to her last son, she tried to name him *Benoni*, meaning *son of my sorrows.* Although Israel (i.e. Jacob) loved Rachel deeply, he refused to let this son be named according to his mother's pain. Instead Israel declared that his son would be named Benjamin – *son of my right hand.*

This became a prophecy of his destiny because Benjamin grew up to be a strong warrior with descendants who were brave fighting men.

Not everyone has such a dramatic story as Benjamin. Therefore, when you are confronted with a name that does not appear to have a positive meaning, be prepared to do a little "detective" work to find the God-story in the name! For example a woman named Wendy, which means *wanderer*, took hold of a new sense of purpose for her name when she was used of God to help those who wander from their faith to return to the Lord.

Another way to bless a name that lacks a positive meaning is to draw upon the character qualities of other people with the same name. A classic example is the name Mary, which comes from the Hebrew word *mara*, meaning *bitter*. It doesn't sound like much of a blessing! However, throughout history many godly women have been named Mary and can be used as positive namesakes, including Mary, Jesus' earthly mother.

For help with preparing a Name Blessing, see Appendix A.

ENDNOTE 1 *Rolf Garborg* (original publication of *The Family Blessing,* pg. 81 Word Publishing. 1990.)

CHAPTER 17

What Single Parent Families Need

Mothers are designed by God to bear and nurture children. A mother is her child's prime source of security and identity in the earliest years of life.

Fathers are designed by God to "call forth" children into their adult identities. During teen years they are to take the lead as a life coach. These complementary roles of parents can be pictured using the metaphor from Psalm 127:4: "Like arrows in the hands of a warrior are sons born in one's youth . . . "

Children arrive in the hands of parents like a stick that must be carefully shaped before it is eventually shot forth to reach its target. A mother focuses upon shaping the bow (the home environment), and the father focuses upon loading the arrow into the bow, aiming and releasing it toward the target.

Most single parent families are led by women. Single moms learn to accept challenges that many two-parent families do not experience. A single mom who is diligent can do a wonderful job on her own to shape an excellent "bow" for her little "arrows" but who will help her fire them toward their target in life?

When children reach teen years, without a father in their life it's difficult for the mother to give the needed blessing on her own. Even if a father is present, if he remains uninvolved in the teenager's life the mother may still find it difficult to give the required blessing without help from her spouse.

When possible, extended families of single parents ought to rally around to help deliver the family blessing (see 1 Timothy 5:4). Here is an example of how well that can work from a single mother whom we coached on blessing her teenage son Jamie:

> *The day of the blessing went extremely well. You had suggested that I ask each person who is close to Jamie to speak blessings in his life in each area outlined in the book. I did, and it was so great to have my parents, my sister and very good friends of the family all speak blessings into Jamie's life for the present and future. Jamie was so touched. He is too "cool" to cry, but I noticed his eyes were filling with tears at one point. It was so powerful to see God at work. We felt His presence without a doubt.*
>
> *Since then so much has happened. My son has more self-confidence than he had before. His grades have improved. His relationships with peers are better and he has stepped up to a leadership role on his basketball team. He became captain of the team, and it has been amazing to see this shy boy blossom to the point where he is giving directions to his team mates. I notice that he is willing to take the initiative in reading the Bible, and he asks for prayer more often now when he has needs. I have to say, it all started with the blessing party last September.*

If no extended family members are available, then it's the duty of the family of God, the Church, to make up for what is lacking. Standing in the "blessing gap" for children who have no father figure can be a wonderful opportunity people to experience the power of God.

A single mother with a son and younger daughter moved to our neighborhood from another country. She was looking for friendship and began to attend our church. Shortly afterward the mom came to faith in Christ, but her 13-year-old son (whom we will call Steve) had little interest in her faith, or in God. During the next seven or eight years there were predictable periods of conflict between the mother and her son, and a few moments of outright rebellion. However, this mom never exhibited self-pity. She worked hard to support her family and integrated herself into the mainstream of church life. She served others and even went on a mission trip. She did everything she could, but she needed help when it came to healthy male role models for her boy. His own father was uninterested in supporting him with words or actions.

During the period when her son was a teen, two or three men, including Terry, decided to make themselves available to mentor Steve. We found reasons to include Steve and his family in social activities in order to provide emotional support and a healthy model of family relationships. On one occasion Terry chartered a boat and took Steve along with our sons on a fishing trip. The owner of the boat was so impressed that he let Steve on board free of charge. Steve's mother also needed blessing. Counselors and friends helped her work through the crucial issues of forgiveness and receive her own missed blessings. By the time Steve was in his early 20s, his mom understood the benefit of giving a Family Blessing even after a child has passed the early stages in life. Steve's mom held a party for him on his birthday and included several adults who had played a significant role in his development.

Here is a portion of the fatherly blessing that Terry prepared to be read on that occasion:

> *Steve, on your birthday, as we reflect on the man you have become and where God will take you, I first want to say that I am proud of you.*
>
> *You had just entered teen years when we first met, and I will never forget watching you wrestle with my eldest son Dave that day and thinking, "I like this boy! He's fun!"*
>
> *You and your mom weathered some difficult times during your teen years, but none of us ever doubted for a minute that you would one day find the inner strength to focus your life upon a worthy goal, and in so doing find purpose and fulfillment.*
>
> *A certain night many years ago as you sat sullenly in the back*

row during a church service, you reluctantly permitted me to pray for you. As I laid my hand on your shoulder, you immediately felt the presence of God, and asked, "What do you have in your hand?"

I found it winsome that you were trying hard not to not participate, but at the same time you were able to sense the presence of God! This was a sign of things to come in your life.

A few years later as you were becoming a man, you were also becoming a man of faith. Your spiritual journey has impacted your friends and family.

You also have a highly developed sense of righteousness which is reflected in your indignation at unfairness of any kind. As you enter your career, I know that you will combine your skill and passion for justice to truly become a man of influence for good.

I believe in you and I am truly excited to see where God will be taking you in the years ahead.

I bless you with open doors – that you will always be in the right place at the right time to take advantage of God's opportunities for your life.

I bless you with spiritual wisdom – that you will always live with a healthy sense of respect for the consequences of all your actions.

I bless your relationships, beginning with your family life and continuing to friendships and business relationships outside your home.

May you always have God's favor as you learn to walk in obedience to the unique life calling that you have been prepared for all these years.

And remember, you do not journey alone. In addition to your family, friends and mentors, I will make myself available to you as often as I can when you need advice or prayer. I consider you a life-long friend and am happy to offer counsel in any circumstance.

Since then Steve moved to another city, graduated from university and is following the Lord's guidance in all that he does. He calls or visits us several times a year, especially when he needs counsel or advice. He openly states that the love of his mom and the influence of two or three male mentors is responsible for the success he enjoys today. That's the kind of help that single parents and their children need.

Blessing single parents and their children

- ***Relationship is a key factor.*** The opportunity to give a spoken blessing flows from a life commitment. Count the cost before you begin. You do not want to raise expectations that you cannot fulfill. Be prayerful in your choice of single parent families alongside whom you will walk.
- ***Set boundaries*** and verbalize the extent of your commitment. Begin slowly so that you don't create unrealistic expectations in your prospect.
- ***Invite a single parent family to join you*** in some of your family events.
- ***A sample blessing*** which you can speak to single mothers is found in Appendix B

For single parents

You may not be able to change your marital status, but you can compensate for the lack of a second parent's blessing in your home:

- ***Be open to your own need for spiritual and emotional health.*** Make it a priority to recover your own missed blessings, and learn to be a good forgiver.
- ***Find a church or small group that welcomes singe parents and their children.*** Do your best to integrate into church life activities.

› ***Get to know those in your circle of touch with a heart for single parents***. These folk are the most likely to become available to assist you in blessing your teens.

› ***Single moms***: if there is no father figure in your children's lives, then *craft the kind of blessing you wish a father would give,* and speak it to them yourself. Regardless of who delivers the blessings during teen years, our heavenly Father can accomplish His work in the lives of your children.

CHAPTER 18

Creative Ideas that Work

We've noticed that nothing stimulates a desire to give and receive blessing more than seeing it in action in other people's lives. When people see it's impact upon others' lives, the light goes on inside and something deep within cries, Me too!

We have compiled a list of stories from ordinary folk who discovered innovative ways to bless their families and others, in hopes that they will inspire you to action. As you read these creative applications, may creative juices flow in your mind and heart. May you be energized to find your own ways to capture this spiritual power and pass it on to the people you love the most.

A blessing "Time Capsule"

A young married couple in our church caught the vision for blessing their two girls. They planned ahead and prepared *years in advance* for a blessing to be given at an important family occasion.

When their eldest daughter was ten years old, they designed a questionnaire that they distributed to their extended family. This form contained questions that guided their family members through the five elements of a blessing, for example: "What is something *you* value about the character qualities of …?" and, "What is the best advice you could give … on her marriage day?"

The mother sealed the responses, and tucked them away for safekeeping until the day they would be used as part of a blessing ceremony at their daughters' wedding receptions.

Only a few months later one of the grandfathers suddenly passed away. At the funeral home, the mother showed us the sealed envelope that her father had returned to her only a few weeks earlier and said, "My father may be gone, but he will still be able to bless his granddaughters on their wedding day!"

A "Back to School Blessing"

Melissa likes to remind parents, "Use any occasion as an opportunity to bless your children!" One family who took her message to heart later sent us the following in an email:

> *My wife and I decided to do an annual blessing ceremony. It usually occurs in September and we call it our "Back to School Blessing."*
>
> *On one occasion, we did it at home. ...everyone gathered on the couch and we had a chair in the middle of the room. Each of the family members took a turn sitting in the chair. I had prepared a written blessing for each of them with a Bible Scripture that suited each one explaining the definition of their name, identifying specific characteristics and personality traits, speaking well of them, and saying something to encourage them for the upcoming school year.*
>
> *Each blessing ended with me saying, "Anytime, anyplace, [for] anything, I'll be there for you.*
>
> *Then I presented each child with a framed photograph of their mother and me, and had them put the blessing behind the photo in the frame so that the blessing stayed with the photo.*
>
> *On another occasion, for our "Back to School Blessing," we had a family portrait taken and then went out to dinner afterwards. At dinner, we presented each child with their blessing for the school year which consisted of a Bible Scripture, identifying specific characteristics and personality traits and speaking well of them, saying something to encourage them for the school year, and [blessing] something about their character."*

Blessing parties for children

Here are two ideas that came from the children's pastor at our church after she began incorporating the concept of blessing into significant events. In her words:

> ***First grade party:*** *Going into first grade is a significant milestone in the lives of children. Starting full days of school can be hard for children (and parents) so we like to celebrate and bless them just before the new school year starts. We normally take them to an indoor party place, and let them have a great time playing and having fun! We not only speak a blessing but seal it with gifts. Each child receives a back-to-school kit of school supplies, and we also get them a devotional book to start off their new school year. This makes them feel really special and is an investment into their lives. We pray over them, and this new season of their life. This has become a really special milestone event for the children in our church entering first grade.*
>
> ***Name Sunday:*** *The meaning of names is also very significant. One idea for a blessing time with children is to make up "name certificates." During a children's ministry time, or even in your own family, you can have helpers look up the meanings of the children's names and the verses that go with their names, and write them down on each certificate. Another idea is then to have people pray for the children individually and bless them and the meaning of their names. I know that after doing this one Sunday, many children (my own son included) were impacted by the meaning of their names. [Their name] became significant to them. It became part of the identity that they were forming for themselves."*

A blessing party for teens

After our daughter returned to her faith God began to bless our children in such a way that within a four month period nearly 20 of their school friends were showing up at church. Most of them made a decision to follow Christ. We have had a lot of fun spending time with these new Christian adolescents and even becoming a "spiritual mom and dad" to a few.

When our son Mark turned 17, we decided to turn his birthday celebration into a blessing party. We invited all of Mark and Jessica's new Christian friends. A dozen of them came. Melissa prepared a name card for each person. On it she wrote the meaning of their name, a spiritual connotation of that meaning, and a related Scripture verse.

Along with typical birthday activities, we spent a few minutes teaching about blessing. Then we gave opportunity for everyone to receive a spoken blessing. *None refused.* We told each one the meaning of their name, and applied it to what we saw in their character. We assured them that they had what it takes to make it in this world, and that it is worth waiting for the right life partner. We also offered to be available for them if and when they needed someone. We laid gentle hands on their shoulders and prayed for God to guide and guard their lives in every way. The cards and calls we received later revealed how much of a lasting impact this event had on these young lives. For some it was the first time in their lives that anyone had given them such affirmation.

Innovations at weddings

At our daughter's wedding we used a white cord which the mothers cut in two as a symbol of releasing our children to their new relationship. The bride and groom each picked up one strand and then braided these together with a third, gold-colored cord representing the Lord Jesus. This provided a powerful visual symbol of a godly marriage, which the Bible describes as "a cord of three strands (which) is not quickly broken" *(Ecclesiastes 4:12).* A verbal blessing by all four parents followed. The wording of this blessing is included in Appendix B.

Thinking BIG in a small town

Pastor Arnie and his wife Ruth had served in a small Canadian town for more than ten years. Having discovered the power of Family Blessing, they held a Name Blessing ceremony for every member of their church. This led them to think of an innovative way to impact their town. In their own words:

> *We had just blessed everyone in the church, finding the meaning of their names.... We decided to do the same for the*

town which would be soon celebrating its 75th anniversary.

Gathering ideas from the town flag, they wrote a blessing on a sheet of parchment and made an appointment to appear before the Town Council.

Arnie read the blessing and Ruth explained the significance of the town's name, "small place of renown." Their effort was warmly received by the Town Council and they hung a copy in the Council Chambers.

Three years later this small Canadian town became the center of nationwide news due to the tragic shooting death of four Royal Canadian Mounted Police officers in the line of duty. In the midst of this tragedy, a message of hope was proclaimed.

The memorial service, held in a local school, was filled with national press and television cameras. Arnie and Ruth were chosen to lead the service and were able to give a clear gospel message of hope in the midst of tragedy. The mother of one of the slain officers publicly urged people to rise above hate and learn to forgive in the name of Jesus Christ.

The name Mayerthorpe became known from coast to coast across our large country. Mayerthorpe more than lived up to the meaning of its name – a small place of renown. It became known not just for tragedy, but also for the manner in which local residents and victims' families responded.

These are just a few ideas flowing from an endless stream of possibilities for applying the power of blessing to your life situations. The appendices that follow contain sample blessings and guides to ensure that you will be able to give a blessing to anyone who needs one. *Never be too shy to give it a try!* Even as a beginner you will be surprised to discover how powerfully God can use your words to bring His blessing into the lives of those you love. We trust that you will take what you have learned and apply it.

Just for you
In conclusion, whatever your family situation *we* want to bless *you!*

The following words come from our hearts and are backed by our prayer to the heavenly Father for everyone who reads the words in this book:

We bless your identity and your destiny*. May you discover the truth of who you are designed to be in Christ and may you rule in your God given area of authority.*

We bless you to go and bless others! *May you give from the overflow of having received more than you can contain.*

May the Lord Bless you
May the Lord bless you and keep you;
May the Lord make His face to shine upon you
And be gracious to you;
May the Lord turn His face toward you and give you peace.
We ask this in Jesus' name. Amen.

Appendix A

How to Craft a Blessing, Prayers and Declarations

Any material in this book is prohibited from being reproduced and included in any form of media which is sold or distributed without written permission from the authors of this book.

Material found in the appendices may be copied or reproduced for your personal non-commercial use.

How to Craft a Blessing for Someone You Know

A blessing has the ability to convey God's favor upon a person when it is crafted with understanding and received with an open heart. Whether spoken or written, the purpose is to recognize and verbalize the noteworthy characteristics of the person and to articulate what you see God may desire to do in their life and through their life in the future.

To help you get started, try following these steps:

› Prayerfully choose a Scripture that conveys a positive message suitable to the person you wish to bless.

› Write a sentence or two describing something noteworthy that you have observed about this person's actions or character.

› Record words that describe this person's value in your eyes and in the sight of God.

› Add any good thing that you perceive God to be doing in their life right now.

› Describe the ways in which you believe this person can be used by God to encourage and bless others in the future.

› If appropriate, state how you are willing to assist this person to achieve the future you have pictured for them.

› *Optional*: Find the meaning of this person's name and incorporate it into the blessing.

How to prepare a Name Blessing

› **Pray** – ask the Lord to reveal His purpose and meaning in the person's name.

› **Research** – look in different sources such as *The Name Book* by Dorothy Astoria. The internet has a plethora of websites that give meanings for names. Research the history of the family name, if desired.

› **Interview** the person to discover a possible "God story" connected to the manner in which they received their name.

› **Select a Scripture** that is compatible with the meaning of the name once you have discovered that meaning. Write a Scriptural connotation in one sentence that links the name with a biblical truth.

› **Prepare a card** or plaque that summarizes the information that you have gleaned.

› **Perform a small name blessing ceremony** that includes presenting the person with their card or plaque (and use the five elements of a Blessing).

› **Conclude the ceremony with a prayer** to "set the seal" of God's love upon their heart through the meaning of their name.

A blessing for someone I know

Name ____

Connect: Delivering the blessing in person is ideal. However, sending a written version to the person can also provide a meaningful connection. How and when I plan to deliver this blessing:

____

____

____

____

Communicate: Record here what you intend to say – see "How to Craft a Blessing for Someone You Know."
A Scripture verse: ______________________________

____

My blessing:

Commit: If appropriate, indicate how you intend to help this person achieve the desired future you have pictured for them:

____

____

____

____

Scriptures suitable for crafting a blessing

Some passages of Scripture, such as Psalm 128, were actually written as blessings. Hundreds more are phrased in such a way as to be easily incorporated into a written or spoken blessing. Below is a small sample just to get you started:

Blessings in Christ	Ephesians 1:3
Chosen by God	Ephesians 1:4,11
Obedience and Long Life	Deuteronomy 5:33 , 30:19,20
Rewards for Kindness	Ruth 2:12
For a Child to Prosper	1 Kings 2:1-3
Family Blessing	Psalm 128
The "marriage bed"	Proverbs 5:18-19
Fertility	Genesis 24:60, Deut 28:11
Prosperity in Business	Deuteronomy 28:1-8, 12-15
Financial Blessing	Deuteronomy 15:10, Psalm 37:25-26, Proverbs19:17, 22:9
Tithing	Malachi 3:10-11
Physical Health	3 John 1
Peace and Holiness	1 Thessalonians 5:23
Wisdom and Revelation	Ephesians 1:17
Wisdom	Proverbs 3:12-18
Spiritual Insight	Ephesians 1:18-19
Spiritual Power	Ephesians 3:15-19
Blessings in Trials	Matthew 5:4,10,11
Spiritual Hunger & Humility	Matthew 5:3,5-9

Don't stop with these!

Now that you understand the idea, as you read the Bible, look for more Scriptures that are written in such a manner as to be suitable to include in any kind of blessing.

Prayers that go with blessing

The forces of Satan and the weaknesses in our human nature

constantly conspire to war against our spiritual growth and advancement. In times of war, every *breakthrough* requires a *follow-through*. The delivery of a spoken blessing can represent a powerful breakthrough in a person's life. Without appropriate follow-through, however, the value of a blessing can be robbed from a person's future experience.

One way to prevent that from happening is to combine times of blessing with a lifestyle of prayer for those we love. Here's a little blessing from us to *you* as you get started:
May your prayers condition the spiritual atmosphere.
May your faith remove mountains of resistance.
May your desires be granted as you make
godly declarations for the people you love.

Daily declaration prayer for the protection and guidance of your family

> *Heavenly Father, I bring my family*
> [INSERT NAMES] *one by one before you.*
>
> *Today I declare in the name of Jesus that my children (and grandchildren)* [INSERT NAMES] *are under your protection, direction, and when necessary, your correction.*
>
> *I place them under the protection and blessing of my believing prayers.*
>
> *In every choice that confronts them, I declare that they will receive wisdom to understand the righteous path and receive the grace to choose that path even if they have not been seeking it.*
>
> *Keep them from all accident, injury and illness.*
>
> *Lead them away from temptation and trial except for the ones you have specifically sent for their growth and for their good.*

Fill them with your Spirit and passion for you. Drain from their soul any love for the world and the things of the world. Give them a spirit of wisdom and understanding in every aspect of their lives.

I declare that no thing, no obstacle or circumstance will prevent them from moving toward their destiny today. Amen.

The following can be added as often as desired where applicable:

Lord I thank you in advance for the marriage of [INSERT NAME]. *I call in your first choice for their life partner. Keep them from him/her until the appointed time and keep them for him/her. Keep their future mate protected from accident, injury and illness. Fill them with your Spirit and a passion to follow you. Keep them from sin and compromise. Lead them away from ungodly relationships and all temptations. Release them to meet* [INSERT NAME] *at the right time.*

Generational blessing prayer

This is not a *daily* declaration, but rather a *one time* prayer of faith. It contains two parts – separation from negative influences and connection to godly heritage. The purpose of this prayer is for you to position yourself spiritually to be more receptive to the full measure of Family Blessing that the heavenly Father has intended for your life.

Before praying this prayer, you may want to consider going on a "treasure hunt" to discover potential blessings that can be inherited from your ancestors. You can begin by filling out your family tree on a chart recalling all the generations for which you have information. Alternately you can list ancestors' names along with any information you feel might be relevant to Family Blessing. Subsequently you can seek out family members from previous generations who are still able to tell the stories of the lives of your relatives from long ago. The more you know about the "God stories" in your family line, the more insight you will have when you pray.

Feel free to expand or modify the format of the following prayer according the insight you receive from your Family Blessing treasure hunt!

In the name of Jesus I separate myself from every negative aspect of my family line. I place the cross of Jesus between me and the lies, cursing, and ungodly relationship patterns from past generations. I declare that I am free to enter into the fullness of my true identity and destiny as planned by my heavenly Father. In faith, I call forward my spiritual heritage in Jesus Christ purchased for me through His death and resurrection. By faith I anticipate receiving the full blessing required to fulfill the Lord's purpose for my generation and also for my descendants. I call for every spiritual blessing from past generations that has not yet been fully released, to be delivered into my life. I ask you, heavenly Father, to reveal and release the full spiritual power that is available to me on this basis. In the name of Jesus, Amen.

Appendix B

Sample Blessings for Ages, Stages, Ceremonies and Celebrations

General Blessings for Each of the Stages

1. ***Conception***	Am I welcome in this world?
2. ***Pregnancy***	Is there a safe place for me in the world?
3. ***Birth***	Will my needs be met in this world?
4. ***Early Childhood***	Who can I trust in this world?
5. ***Teen Years***	Do I have what it takes to make it in this world?
6. ***Adulthood***	What am I called to do in this world? Who will share my journey?
7. ***Senior Years***	Am I still needed in this world?

Examples of life-stages blessings

The following blessings are designed to be a starting point from which you can build a uniquely special blessing for someone you love.

Your Earth Day – life begins at conception:

> ***We bless the day of your conception.*** *Welcome to this world!*
>
> ***We bless your uniqueness.*** *You are God's choice. Out of the hundreds of millions of possible combinations from your parents' DNA, God determined that you would be you.*
>
> ***We bless the timing of your arrival on earth.*** *You were no accident. God wanted you here for this time and for His purpose and so He gave permission for your spirit to be made alive on earth at exactly the right time regardless of the human circumstances.*
>
> ***We bless the destiny that was pre-planned for your life.*** *Before the foundation of the earth, you existed in the mind and heart of God. All the days of your life were ordained before one of them came to be* (see Psalm 139:16). *May you*

discover the sheer joy of walking in the steps that God has ordered for your life.

We bless your eternal home. *The same Heavenly Father who sent your spirit to earth is waiting to welcome you back to Himself one day. May your stay on earth include a rich personal relationship with Jesus Christ while He prepares a place in heaven just for you* (see John 14:2).

Your pre-born days:

We bless your pre-born days, *when you were uniquely crafted and specifically designed for God's purpose.*

We bless the formation of your body, *that God performed in secret while you waited to be released to this world* (see Psalm 139:13-15).

We bless your emotional life, *that you may understand deep in your heart that God will always provide a safe place for you, a place of refuge on this earth from the forces that set themselves against you. May God's perfect love displace any fears in your life.*

(A full pregnancy blessing is found later in this section)

Your birthday:

We bless the day of your birth. *May your know that your needs will always be met according to God's supply.*

We bless your gender, *for you were created to be a man/ woman, according to God's design.*

We bless your birth order, *in the family to which you were given. May the timing of your arrival and the relationships with family members be used by God to perfect you according to His will.*

We bless your mental growth, as you begin to process the world around you. May your ear gates and eye gates be guarded by those who care for you and keep you in their home.

We bless your spiritual journey. *May it begin with a dedication to a faith community that follows Jesus Christ. May you be spiritually protected by people and by God's angels from all harm and deception until you are old enough to make your own choices.*

We bless your name. *May God lead your parents to choose a name with a meaning suited to your identity and destiny. May God's purpose for your name be revealed and fulfilled as you grow up.*

Your early childhood:

We bless your early childhood, that you may learn to trust everyone who exercises godly authority in your life.

We bless your play times, that you may learn and grow to your full potential. May you be kept safe at all times.

We bless your mental development, that nothing would hinder the growth of your mind to its full potential.

We bless the development of your will, that you may be shaped in wisdom and love by those in authority in your life. May you learn to make wise choices in every life decision.

We bless your spiritual life, that you would understand and experience what it means to walk with God at a young age.

We bless your family relationships, that you would discover and enjoy a sense of belonging in a family that loves you. May you be kept safe from accidental emotional injury and improper discipline.

We bless your school experiences. May school be a safe place for you to learn and grow. May school authorities recognize and encourage your gifts and talents.

We bless your friendships. May you may be guided to make wise choices in every relationship outside your family circle.

Your teen years:

We bless your teen years. *You have what it takes to fulfill everything God has called you to do. As you apprentice for adulthood, may your unique talents and gifts be recognized, encouraged and developed in preparation for your life's work.*

We bless your physical development, *that you would be content and happy in the body God has given you as it reaches maturity. May you enjoy excellent health.*

We bless your mental development, *that you will receive the necessary education and intellectual preparation for your life's work. May you appreciate both the process and outcome of learning.*

We bless you spiritually, *that you may have personal encounters with living God. May you experience consistent growth in your faith, day by day. May you be given the strength to resist temptation. May you learn to hear the voice of God's Spirit. May you develop a devotional habit of prayer and Bible reading that lasts a lifetime.*

We bless you socially, *that you may experience true friendships, a good reputation, and a safe environment in which you feel loved and accepted for who you are.*

We bless your need to grow. *May you learn from your mistakes and experiment with your gifts and talents. May you never fear to accept new challenges and test the limits of your capabilities within the boundaries set by godly authority.*

For a ceremony such as a Bar/Bat Barakah you may want to add:

Today I call you forth into manhood/womanhood.
You are no longer a child.
You are now an emerging adult.
I am proud to be your father/mother
You have what it takes to become a man/woman of great character.
You are unconditionally loved and never need to prove your worth or value through your own efforts.
You have everything you need to find and fulfill your destiny.
I commit myself to support you in every way (time, finances, counsel, prayers) during this exciting journey.

Your adult years:

We bless your adult identity and your destiny in this world.
May you discover the purpose for which God sent you to this earth and 'rule' in your God given area of authority. May you learn God's ways and discern God's paths as you fulfill God's purpose for your life.
May you always follow the leading of God's Spirit in every decision you face.
May you never stop growing in the understanding and application of God's Word for your life.

***We bless your marriage,**. that what God has joined together, no one would ever separate. May your life mate be your closest friend and most understanding companion. May you walk together in unity spiritually as well as emotionally.*
Or May you meet and marry God's perfect choice as a life partner...

***We bless your children,** that the generational blessing upon your family line would be passed on to them. May each child provide breadth and depth to your own life experience. May each one share your values in life and experience a personal walk with God.*

We bless your relationships, *that God would lead you to those who can mentor you as well as those who need to receive from what you have been given. May you never be without meaningful friendships.*

We bless your finances, *that you may always enjoy God's provision. We bless the work of your hands, that your industry and labour will bring abundance to provide for your family and to sow into the lives of others. May you discern how to be an excellent steward of your resources in every situation. May you live securely without need or fear of want. May you learn to be content within the limits of God's provision.*

We bless your health, *that you may be physically capable of every task set before you by God, and not succumb to sickness. May you be kept from injury and illness. May you prosper physically even as your soul prospers.*

We bless your Christian witness, *that you would carry with you the fragrance of Christ in all that you do. May your character and lifestyle be a witness to the truth of God's promises. May you have many opportunities to share your personal faith and bear much fruit as you continue to abide in the Vine, Jesus Christ.*

We bless you to go and bless others! *May you give from the overflow of having received more than you can contain.*

Your senior years:

We bless your senior years, *that you may continue to find a place of significance and purpose in this world. May you discover that you are needed and wanted by those of us who follow after you.*

We bless your life's work. *May you receive appropriate honor for your years of labour. May your contribution to the Kingdom* *of God on this earth be recognized and blessed.*

We bless your life transition *from working in the field to sitting in the gates. May you be sought out for wisdom and counsel so that your hard earned insights will benefit many in the years and generations to come.*

We bless your health, *that your strength will match the length of your days. May you be kept from accident, injury and illness.*

We bless your relationship *with your children that they may rise up and call you blessed. As you become less able to look after your own needs, may they be more available to care for you.*

Special blessings for Baby
Pregnancy Blessing: by Melissa Bone

For Mom:

I (or we) bless this pregnancy.
You are the right mom for this child... this baby is in the right body.
I bless your body as you grow this little one inside. May the Lord "strengthen your frame" (see Isaiah 58:11) *and give you a strong back to carry this child to full term. God has ordained for you to be its mother and you will be a good one.*
You have what it takes to raise this child, with God's help. He has overshadowed you, and what is conceived in you has been accomplished by the will of God and the help of the Holy Spirit.
May your baby come into the light in the fullness of time, not too late or too early!
I bless your labour and delivery, that it would be smooth and free of complications.
I bless you with good health, strength and peace - no fear of the future.
I call you blessed among women! Blessed is the fruit of your

womb, blessed is this child you are bearing. And blessed is she who has believed that what the Lord has said to her will be accomplished (see Luke 1:42-45)*!*

For baby:

I bless you baby. Welcome to this world.
You are in the right body, and you are right on time.
You were supposed to be born at this time in history, and to these parents (or this mother if a single mom).
I call you a blessed child. You are the right gender.
I bless your development, the organs and systems that are in place now.
God is putting the finishing touches on you now… (depending on where the mother is in her gestation, I will often 'bless' what I know to be going on at her the stage in her trimester)
I bless you to 'stay put' until the fullness of time.
I bless you to not come too early or too late, but right on time.
I call your birthday a blessed day, when you come from the darkness into the light.
I bless you in Jesus' name!

This unique ceremony was designed by a young married couple who desired to incorporate blessing into a traditional church baby baptism ceremony from their families of origin.

Baby/child dedication:

There is no one like you on the face of the earth.
I bless your gender. May you be glad that God has decided that you are to be a boy/girl.
I bless your mind to understand the plans God has for you
I bless your heart to know that you are God's unique gift to the world.
I bless your ears to hear the voice of the God's Spirit.
I bless your eyes to see your world the way God sees it
I bless your mouth to give praise to God and blessing to people
I bless your feet to walk in the paths chosen for you by your Heavenly Father

I bless your natural talents and your spiritual gifts. May you discover and develop them at an early age.
May everyone who looks after you in your childhood be kind and loving.
May your heart and mind be protected harsh words and lies.
May you love God with all you heart, mind and strength.
May you always choose your friends wisely.
May you discover God's first choice for a life partner.
May you find and fulfill your life's calling.
May you have God's provision and be kept in good health at every age and stage of your life.

The blessing is followed by the prayer of dedication which also invokes God's blessing upon the child:

Dear heavenly Father, today we offer back to you the precious gift named [INSERT CHILD'S NAME] *that you have given to* [INSERT PARENTS' NAMES].
I stand in agreement together with the family members to ask in faith that you would keep [INSERT CHILD'S NAME] *under your protection, direction and when necessary correction all the days of his/her life. We ask that he/she would come to know Jesus Christ as personal Savior at an early age and that he/she would become acquainted with the presence and power of the Holy Spirit. May he/she also love the family of God and always be in fellowship with a healthy church congregation.*
May [INSERT CHILD'S NAME] *be kept from unnecessary trials and temptations.*
We ask that you give the parents spiritual wisdom and revelation about the unique identity and destiny of this child.
We ask that you would guide them in learning how to bless him/her at every age and stage.
May he/she be enabled to prosper in every area of his/her life.
We invoke your presence and power upon him/her so that everything we ask will be accomplished .
In the name of Jesus Christ, Amen.

Baby/child dedication ceremony with blessing:

a) Introduction:

It is our wonderful privilege today to participate in the public dedication of [INSERT CHILD'S NAME].
(Read Luke 2:22b–40.)

A month after Jesus' birth, He was blessed on His first trip to the temple. God had two seniors specially prepared to recognize Him by the Spirit. Both Simeon and Anna blessed baby Jesus and spoke prophetically about His identity and destiny.

The blessing at birth includes the naming and dedication, or baptism of the baby. Regardless of which tradition parents follow, the parent's faith, rather than the child's faith, is active. Baptism, or dedication, brings the child under God's protection and activates the unfolding of God's plan for their life.
The three elements of dedication are

- *to teach and train the child with the principles of God's Word*
- *to seek to lead the child to a saving faith in Jesus Christ at an early age*
- *to provide godly examples by their own lives*

Dedication is as much, or more about the parents, God-parents, family and friends than it is the children. It is a sacred covenant from God given to the parents and the immediate family in trust that they will act on His behalf to care for and raise His child – a precious gift to whom they are also meant to impart identity and destiny. It does take a community to raise a child!

Jesus demonstrated His acceptance and love for little children when He said, "Let the little children come to me, and do not hinder them, for the kingdom of God belongs to such as these. And He took the children in His arms, put His hands on them, and blessed them," (see Mark 10:14,16).

b) Call parents to come to front of room with child: Name meaning – read by mother or father.

c) Charge to parents:

The primary responsibility for the care of_______, rests on the parents. Scripture says:

- *"Train up a child in the way he should go and when he is old, he will not depart from it."*
- *"Bring them up in the nurture and admonition of the Lord."*
- *"These commandments that I give you today are to be upon your hearts. Impress them on your children. Talk about them when you sit at home and when you walk along the road, when you lie down and when you get up."*

_______________________, as you engage in this task with joy and peace, may you earnestly seek the Lord daily for His wisdom for all the events that will occur, all the decisions to be made and all the needs to be met. For as James says, "If any of you lack wisdom, he should ask God, who gives generously to all without finding fault, and it will give to him."

May you also daily give thanks to God for your child and for the joy and love she brings to your home.

d) Charge to the God-parents:

Based on the Scripture we read about Jesus' dedication, the parents have chosen two special people, like Simon and Anna, to be God parents.

__________ will have the benefit of the influence provided by her God parents, who are being asked to provide backup support for her spiritual training.

It is your responsibility to provide a caring, supportive group for this family. I ask you to be faithful in prayer for them, and undergird their efforts to establish a strong home built on Christian principles. I urge you to demonstrate a real interest in and concern for ______as she grows physically, mentally, socially and spiritually.

[INSERT GOD PARENTS NAMES] *do you promise to love, support and pray for _________? Do you promise to encourage and pray for ______ and ______ as they raise _________? To be a support and help whenever you are needed?*

e) Charge to the family:

There is one other important support system for _________, the extended family. At this time members of this family may stand to evidence the acceptance of their part of this responsibility. I charge you to do all that you can to provide and support a place of love and safety where _________ may know that he is welcome and accepted for the unique individual God created him to be. I urge you to provide appropriate affectionate love and kindness towards all of your little ones in the ______________families. And I charge you to covenant before God to set an example by your lives and to maintain an atmosphere in your homes that will inspire _________ to be successful in life and to find his identity and destiny – fulfillment and purpose for the future. Do you promise to love, encourage, support and pray for _________? If so answer "we do."

f) Commitments:

And now, ______ and ______, in the sight of God and in the presence of these witnesses,

› *Do you solemnly undertake to bring up _________ in the knowledge and grace of the Lord, Jesus Christ? If so answer "we do."*
› *Do you promise, to the best of your ability, to set before your son examples of consistent Godly living?*

› *Do you promise to love, protect, nurture and train _________ so that he will grow up to be loving and truthful, an asset to whatever community you live in?*

Do you promise to tell him about God, Jesus His Son and the Holy Spirit?

g) Blessing by the father: ______

h) Anointing of oil: God parents hold baby.
Head – Romans 12, 1,2
Hands – Proverbs 3:16
Feet – Psalm 121:3

i) The God parents have a special gift for the child – a gold cross.

The gold cross is a reminder to us to do as Jesus said in Luke 9:23: "If anyone would come after me, he must deny himself and take up his cross daily and follow me."

j) The pastor receives the child from the God parents:

And now, on the authority of God's Holy Word, and as a minister in Christ's church, I dedicate you, _______, unto the Lord, and unto His service, according to His will.

k) Father's blessing:

Dear___________:
We celebrate your life. You are a God's gracious gift to us. We bless your gender and birth order in our family. We bless you to grow to become healthy, beautiful and strong. We bless you to be godly, seeking after God's heart and desiring to walk with God at a young age and live a righteous life. We bless you to be successful in every aspect of life – spiritually, physically, mentally, socially and financially. We bless every stage of your life – from your childhood to teen years to adulthood, that you would choose the right career and life partner.

May you know that you are welcomed, loved and accepted in our family.

Ideas for blessing your young child:

Here are three ways the power of blessing has been incorporated in the children's ministry by the staff at our church. *If you are not in a ministry or church setting*, these are things that you could incorporate into family traditions, or even join with some other parents and do them together.

First grade party: Going into grade one is a huge milestone that we like to celebrate in the lives of children. Starting full days of school can be hard for children (and parents) so we like to celebrate and bless them just before the new school year starts. This is a great relationship and connecting time for children and families. We take them to an indoor party place and let them have a great time playing and having fun. We bless each child with a back-to-school kit of school supplies, and we also get them a devotional book to start off their new school year. This makes them feel really special and it is a spiritual investment into their lives. We pray over them and this new season of their life. This has become a really special milestone event for the children in our church entering grade one.

Special girl and boy events: How about celebrating children just for who they are? Special events can really make it meaningful in the lives of children.

For little girls, you can host a princess tea party where you teach them that they are daughters of the King and therefore royalty. This is a great time to celebrate their girlhood and make them feel special and beautiful inside and out.

Another idea is a girl's spa/slumber party where they come in their pj's. You do their nails and hair and teach them about beauty inside and out.

Events like these will stay will little girls forever and impact their futures.

Boys are different (obviously!) Celebrating boys involves loud and messy events. Outdoor scavenger hunts or water wars, even a giant video game night are great ideas creating events where boys can bond with each other. Let them release their energy and just be themselves with other boys. Boys want to let loose and just have fun – so bless to do it. Celebrate boyhood!

Name Sunday: Celebrating the meaning of names is very significant. One idea for a significant blessing time with children would be to make up "name certificates." During a children's ministry time or even in your own family, you can have helpers look up the meanings of the names of the children, and the verse that goes with their name. Write them down on the certificate. Another idea is to have people pray for the children individually and bless them and the meaning of their names. Knowing the meaning of their names can influence children powerfully in the formation of their sense of identity.

Examples of life-stages blessings, teen to senior years

A blessing for a new teen based upon Luke 2:52:

> (Read Luke 2:52 aloud). *Jesus had God's favor and therefore He matured in four ways as He entered teen years – mentally, socially, physically and spiritually.*
>
> *Over these seven years, you will leave behind childhood and become an adult. Even now your new identity is emerging. I bless you to receive God's favor in the following ways:*
>
> ***I bless the development of your mind****: For the first 12 years of your life, your brain has been growing. One trillion cells have been added since your life began. The growth of your brain is now complete, but not the growth of your mind. May you increase in knowledge and in wisdom. May you come to know your gifts and talents and learn to how to use them for good. May lies be recognized and rejected and truth be recognized and received.*
>
> ***I bless your physical development****: May you grow strong*

and always be in good health.
May you be happy with the physical attributes God has given you and use your strength to serve Him.

I bless your social development:
May you receive appropriate recognition for your emerging identity from your parents as well as teachers and other authority figures.
May you continue to submit to godly authority figures.
May you have the strength to say NO to negative peer pressure.
May you always have meaningful and healthy friendships during teen years; may some of these friendships last a lifetime!

I bless your spiritual development:
May you develop real wisdom by listening to the advice of your parents, and always thinking about the consequences of your actions.
May you have spiritual experiences that will positively impact you for the rest of your life.
May you have a love for the Word of God and a growing knowledge of how it applies to your life.
(Read Psalm 19:9-11).

A wedding blessing:

This blessing was written by Terry and Melissa Bone for their own daughter's wedding. It was included in the actual wedding ceremony. The officiating minister took a moment to explain the purpose and the meaning of a blessing and then invited the parents of both the bride and the groom to come forward and stand beside their child – with one hand extended (or gently touching) the child's shoulder. As the minister read the blessing phrase by phrase, the parents repeated it aloud in unison phrase by phrase. It was followed by hugs and kisses all around (with parents being very careful not to ruffle the bride's make-up or dress!).

We call this day a blessed day for all of us.
We recognize the eternal plan of God in bringing each of us to this momentous occasion.

We acknowledge that it is God's grace that has prepared you for this day from birth.
We bless your choice of life partner and we believe that you are God's first choice for each other. We release you from our home with our blessing.
We bless the establishing of your own home together.
We commit ourselves to be available for counsel and assistance whenever you call upon us.
We commit ourselves to pray for you often trusting the Holy Spirit to prompt us.
May God guide your every step so that you may fulfill His highest purpose for your lives.
May God provide for your every need at every stage of your journey together.
May you be blessed with children of your own in God's perfect timing.
May the same blessing that you have received today/ be passed on to your children and grandchildren.

A blessing for Single Parents

May your home be blessed with the peace and presence of God
May your children be guarded and guided by angels at every moment they are with you and beyond your sight
May you have the grace to endure the extra workload of single parenting and to avoid self pity when you feel alone
May your need for authentic friendship be fulfilled as God brings people into your life who have genuine interest in your well being
May you be favored financially so that your labor will adequately provide for your family
May your family circle be unbroken when you get to heaven

A blessing for Single Parents based upon The 'Beatitudes' (from the famous 'Sermon on the Mount', Matthew chapter 5)

Blessed are you when you feel poor in spirit – when you have come to the end of your own strength for in that moment you are in possession of a priceless treasure – the knowledge that apart from Jesus you can do nothing.

Blessed are you when you mourn over relationships that could have been. For in such times you can identify with Christ's sufferings and He will comfort you.

Blessed are you when you are meek – when you quietly accept the financial challenges without a spouse to assist you – for God has not forgotten your situation and He will supply your needs.

Blessed are you when you hunger and thirst for your children to follow the Lord for in time your desire shall be fulfilled.

Blessed are you when you are merciful with your children. For through you they will see God's heart and experience His love and forgiveness.

Blessed are you when your greatest desire is God's will for your family – for you will find Him showing up in unexpected ways when you need Him most.

Blessed are you when you refuse to act vengefully or speak negatively when you are mistreated by a former spouse, for through this , peace will reign in your home.

Blessed are you when you are misunderstood, misjudged or neglected by those who have never had to walk in your shoes. For He who sees in secret, will one day reward you openly.

Blessed will be your home as you call upon the Name of the Lord. For the heart of He who defends the widow and the orphan shall also be touched by your heart's cry.
May God Bless Single Parents.

A blessing for a son on his wedding day:

We bless you today on this your wedding day. Since the day we knew of your conception we have loved and cherished you.

You have always been loved, wanted and welcome in our lives and in our hearts. The Lord blessed us with you, a wonderful son.
We bless you today as a bridegroom and rejoice with you in the celebration of your love and commitment to ________, your wife.
We bless you as a husband to take leadership and be the spiritual head of your family.
Our prayers for you since you were little is that you would become a "mighty man of God."
May the Lord give you wisdom and discernment so that you may become a good and loving husband.
May the Lord give you faithfulness, strength and a love that will always honor ________ by preferring her needs over your own.
May the Lord give you a love for His Word, His truth and a heart to pray for your wife and children.
May the Lord give you courage, boldness and strength of character to establish godly boundaries and activities that will bless and nurture your loved ones.
May the Lord bless you and ________ with a child of your union and may the generational blessings that have flowed through our family continue to flow through you.
May the Lord give you good parenting skills and the wisdom required to be a godly father.
May you be a good listener and never tire of blessing your children with quality time, words and caring actions.
We commit to love and pray for you and your family, to be there whenever you need us.

***A blessing for a daughter-in-law on her* wedding day:**

________ we welcome you into the _____ family. We bless this day of new beginnings.
Over the past ___ years we have come to know you as a friend whom we love and cherish.
You are physically beautiful and radiant today. We bless the beauty of your heart and your soul as well.
We bless you as our daughter-in-law and our friend. We bless

you as a bride and rejoice with you as the two of you have vowed before God to love, honor and cherish one another all the days of your lives.
May your marriage relationship be filled with all God's good and perfect gifts that He has in mind for you both. We bless you as a wife. May the Lord give you unconditional love, patience, wisdom, strength and discernment for the journey that lies ahead of you.
May your relationship with __________grow stronger and sweeter and even more precious as you purpose in your heart to honor God and your husband.
May the Lord prosper you and _______and give you favor with your employers, your family and give you godly friends. We commit to pray for you and to be there whenever you need us or ask for our help.
May the Lord give you a home, a place that has space and room to live, grow and play. _____________we rejoice over you and celebrate with you.

A 25th wedding anniversary blessing:

Parts of this blessing could also be adapted for someone reaching their 25th birthday.

This blessing was given by Terry and Melissa Bone to a husband and wife who reached their 25th anniversary shortly after the both came to know Jesus Christ as their Savior.

Our lives are a story written by the hand of God. Truly God knows how the last chapter will end before the first chapter begins.

"_______ and ________, your story so far has included many years of God's unseen hand leading and guiding you even before you recognized his involvement in your lives. Then, having met Him personally, you discovered the joy of watching God fill in the blanks of your life story – the experience of looking back and recognizing God's sure hand of guidance.

You have learned to honor God, not out of fear but out of love and respect for His ways in your life. And He has already answered many of your prayers.

We rejoice in what He has done in your lives and we stand with you at this juncture as you say, so far so good.

You are about to enter the time of your lives! The number 25 is perhaps more significant than just a milestone along the way – more than just a flag we wave above our marriage to prove we have above average ability to endure.

I looked up the number 25 in the Bible to see what, if any mention there might be. I discovered that no less than five Kings of Israel began their ministry at the age of 25 years (see 2 Chronicles 25:1, 27:1, 29:1, 36:5 and 2 Kings 14:2). *Each of them were good kings! It seems that God feels that 25 years is often what it takes to mature people for future service. One of those kings was a man named Jotham. His name means "God is perfect," literally, complete and pure. The Bible uses the following words to describe Jotham's reign:*

"Jotham grew powerful because he walked steadfastly before the Lord his God" (2 Chronicles 27:6).

The Hebrew phrase in this verse translated grew powerful can mean any of the following:

- *to prevail, to become strong or firm*
- *to be courageous, to be resolute*
- *to cure, help, repair, fortify.*

This is our blessing to you today:

May you be like King Jotham in every way:

- *in his name - may you never lose sight of the fact that God's ways are complete in your life*
- *may you be steadfast – never moved from the confidence of what you know to be true*

- *may you grow powerfully so that – you prevail in every trial. Become strong through every test, be courageous in every danger, become firm in your understanding, never stubborn but resolute in your commitment to each other*
- *may your lives and especially your marriage be what causes others to acquire hope and to become strong and be fortified*
- *may your words and your actions help to cure and repair broken lives, introducing them to their Savior and guide*
- *may your children know their God because of the demonstration of His faithfulness in your lives.*

This blessing was followed by a time of prayer.

A blessing for my friend Wayne on his 50th birthday (by Terry Bone):

Wayne I thank God for you. I thank God for the way you seek your heavenly Father and to do His will. I am inspired to see your love for your wife and family and your passion for ministry. I love to see your sensitivity to the Holy Spirit and your excitement about the Kingdom of God and all its manifestations in our world. You really do get excited about what God is doing not only in your life but in others around you.

Middle age is bursting with potential. By this stage in life a man often has accumulated something in his financial storehouse, no longer has children at home and has enough health and maturity to do something great with his life. In spite of this, the opportunities presented to a middle aged man are more often than not squandered to one degree or another. These years represent one of the most dangerous times in life – especially when we have achieved some of our earlier life goals. Our minds, bodies and surrounding culture can deceive us into adopting a sense of entitlement where we feel we have paid our dues in a number of areas and now it is our turn to relax and enjoy. People in their middle age can easily fail to notice how much the next generation needs their wisdom, encouragement and prayers. Consequently many middle aged men back off from the cutting edge, fail to develop a new vision for the future and slowly but surely become less outward focused, turning their heart toward vacations and material pursuits, and slowing down in their spiritual growth.

Wayne I believe that this is not the path you will take. I believe that you will achieve your God given destiny and use your middle age to position yourself for life long success. And so I call upon the Spirit of God to invest His power and presence into these words:

› ***I bless your middle years*** *that you will never lose your passion for God and your desire to achieve significant accomplishments for His sake.*

› ***I bless your work*** *– may you have favour with your employer. May you have peace in your current career circumstances and grace to use it as a tool for the Kingdom of God.*

› ***I bless your marriage and family*** *– may you all enjoy excellent health and spur each other on to good works.*

› ***I bless your spiritual life*** *– may you experience the pure joy of The Heavenly Father's unconditional love and approval – may you personally hear His words "You are my beloved son in whom I am well pleased."*

› ***I bless your friendships*** *– may you have significant male friends who inspire you and keep you accountable and may you become a mentor as well as a friend to younger men.*

› ***I bless your ministry*** *– may God expand the borders of your influence and increase the fruitfulness of your labours in every task to which you put your hand.*

› ***I bless your spiritual perception and insight*** *– may you have revelation to understand where the borders are being set at each phase of your life – so that you may occupy to the limits (but no further) of God's grace and provision. So that you would be able to say with David "the* ***boundary lines*** *have fallen for me in pleasant places; surely I have a delightful inheritance"* (see Psalm 16:6).

As the Lord brings you to mind I will continue to pray for you as Paul prayed for his friends in Ephesus (see Ephesians 3). *I pray that out of His glorious riches He may strengthen you with power through His Spirit in your inner being; power to overcome temptation – the lust of the eyes, the lust of the flesh, and the pride of life; power to overcome frustration at the imperfections of people and the world around you, power to recognize and reject the lies that the enemy uses against you; power to endure the inevitable trials and setbacks that surprise us along the way.*

I pray this so that you, being rooted and established in love, may have power, together with all the saints, to grasp how wide and long and high and deep is the love of Christ, and to know this love that surpasses knowledge – that you may be filled to the measure of all the fullness of God.

A retirement blessing (based on Proverbs 31:23):

In biblical times, people worked in the fields outside the city and came inside the gates at night for protection. Upon retirement from regular labour seniors were often asked to sit in the gates as a sign of honor and to keep watch over the affairs of the city.

Interesting to note: In Old Testament times, Levites (who looked after the temple) were commanded to cease regular labour at 50 years of age and to begin mentoring the newly appointed 25-year-old Levites (see Numbers 8:23-26).

Today we honor your ___ years of labour/service in

__________________________.

We bless your transition from laboring in your chosen field to "sitting in the gates."
May this gift of time become an opportunity for continual personal growth.
May you always be a good steward of your time.
May you find purpose and fulfillment in your new and different role in life.
May others seek you for your wisdom.
May you become a mentor to younger men/women in the

same profession.
May you always be held in honor by your family and peers.

A blessing for senior parents (written by the children of Christian parents):

In Proverbs 31:28, the children of the virtuous woman rise up to call her blessed.
We want to take this opportunity to honor and bless you for your character and virtuous deeds throughout your life.

For added effect, those speaking the blessing, can begin in a seated position and stand to their feet as they begin the next sentence:

Today we rise up and call you blessed ...
We honor you for the years of selfless service spent in raising your children; for providing for our material, emotional and spiritual needs.
We honor you for preferring our needs over your own and for the sacrifices you made for our sake.
We honor your commitment to following the Lord Jesus and bless you for imparting your spiritual values to us.
We honor you for providing Godly role model(s) to follow.
We are blessed and inspired by your integrity.
We thank you for your many prayers that have guarded us from unseen troubles.
We thank you for imparting your wisdom and teaching us valuable life lessons.
We thank you for being available for us in the following ways ...

At this point some brief stories about the couple can be shared in the blessing.

For the remaining years that God grants you to remain upon earth

May you never be without the presence of the Holy Spirit.
May your heart always be at peace.

May your mind always be alert and learning.
May your strength match the length of your days.
May God keep you in His love at all times.

We bless your memories that you may recall the goodness of God and the great times had with family and friends.

We bless your spiritual life, that you may continue to worship God in spirit and in truth.

We commit ourselves to walk with you for the rest of your journey on earth.

During the sunset years of your life, as you become less able to care for yourselves, we will become more available to help look after your needs…

Or if separated by distance

…to visit when we are able and to pray for you when we cannot be near you.

As you look upon your children today, you are also looking at the beginning of a legacy that will last for generations.

We commit ourselves to carry forward your legacy and pass on our spiritual heritage to our children and grandchildren.

Finish with the Aaronic blessing.

A house blessing:

"Every good and perfect gift is from above, coming down from the Father of the heavenly lights..." (James 1:17, NIV).

A house dedication is an act of gratitude and recognition that God is the source and sustainer of all good things.

We bless this house as a good and perfect gift from God our Father. It is God's choice for our family both in structure and in location. We bless the neighborhood and the relationships we shall form while living here.

A house dedication is an act of consecration – inviting the presence of God's Spirit to dwell with the family in this home.

We bless this house, that it may be a dwelling place of the Holy Spirit whom we now invite to dwell among us, to guard us guide us, teach us and convict us when we stray from the path of honor and family blessing.

We declare the cornerstone of this house to be Jesus Christ. (Read 1 Peter 4:2-8).

A house dedication is an act of protection. It is an acknowledgement that God will be the protector of this family and their home against those forces that rob their peace or possessions. It is a request to keep the structure and its occupants safe from fire and other dangers.

Father God we ask for your protection upon this home. Set your angels to guard the four corners of this property. May there never be any unauthorized access. May nothing ever be taken or stolen from this house. May you keep us safe.